Germany's U-85
<u>A Shadow in The Sea</u>

"Enemy submarines are to be called U-boats; the term submarines is to be reserved for allied underwater vessels. U-boats are those dastardly villains who sink our ships, while submarines are those gallant and noble craft which sink theirs."

Winston Churchill

Spade Fish swim above the conning tower of U-85.

U-85
A Shadow In
The Sea

JIM W. BUNCH

Kriegsmarine u-boat medal, U-bootsabzeichen
Award after three WWII operational patrols.

Deep Sea Press
Nags Head, North Carolina

Copyright 2003 by Jim Bunch
All rights reserved, including the right to reproduce this book or portions thereof in
any form whatsoever. Contact the author with reference to permissions.

International Standard Book Number 0-939591-00-6
Library of Congress Catalog Card No. 86-71436

Published by
Deep Sea Press
Nags Head, North Carolina

U-85 A Shadow in the Sea is the first of a
three part series about the U-85 submarine.
Part two, Records and Reports, and part three,
U-85, A Pictorial History, are being
prepared for publication.

Distributed by
Deep Sea Press
P. O. Box 7301
Kill Devil Hills, North Carolina 27948

Cover photograph of U-85 entering St. Nazaire, February 23, 1942

Fourth Printing 2014
Printed in the Hong Kong

CONTENTS

Preface

Out in the Atlantic where the southernmost eddies of the cold Labrador Current endlessly meander between the warm clear waters of the Gulf Stream and the North Carolina coastline, a lone German U-boat, the U-85, lies today on a patch of seafloor slowly rusting away in the salt water. Her sudden metamorphous from a fighting submarine in Hitler's *Kriegsmarine* to a refuge for marine life was harsh and came quickly. For more than 50 years now, this gray raider from the past, and only 20 miles from the American coastline, continues to be a silent reminder of how close the U-boats were during the early days of 1942.

For years, I have had a special interest in this submarine and the stories that surround her. At first, curiosity took me there, but the adventure, mystery, and just plain fun of exploring a sunken U-boat have always compelled me to return. Ten stories down beneath the often rough and dangerous waters of the Atlantic, U-85 still gives me what most true wreck divers seek, an unpredictable environment and the endless chance of discovery.

Over the past 20 summers, I have ventured out to the U-85 more than 500 times. Each trip has been special. No two dives or boat rides were ever the same. My diving logs always bring back happy memories and the adventures of days gone by. Art Lepage, John Finelli, Kevin Bradshaw, John A. Watkins, Lionel Shannon, Rich and Roger Hunting, Billy Daniels, Phil McGrath, and Larry Keen are just a few of the great friends I was lucky enough to dive with here.

In 1986, I wrote and published a book, *Diving the U-85*. The following revised account hopefully provides a more complete and historically accurate story of this U-boat. The photos, historical background material, diagrams, and personal recollections have been compiled after many years of research and diving. I would like to thank all who helped me with this challenging task.

Built as a weapon of war by a government that no longer exists and gone as a threat to our way of life before I was born, U-85 will continue to be a focus for divers and historians. The adventure there will never end until the last dive is made on the U-85, and the wreck finally dissolves in the seawater that surrounds her.

Acknowledgements

I would like to thank the following individuals for their help in making this book become a reality:

Roger and Rich Hunting for help with the pictures and for taking me to the U-85 so many times.

Gary Gentile for advice about publishing and the use of his files.

Bill Hughes and John Finelli for use of their photos and files.

Wolfgang Klaue for pictures and much technical information about the U-85.

Ed Caram for technical information and use of his photographs.

Michael A. deCamp for use of his underwater photographs.

Larry Keen and Phil McGrath for technical help and trips on the *Gekos*.

Glen Eure for his paintings and sketches.

Bev Kearns for encouragement

David Hamer for photos and technical information about *enigma*.

Homer Hickam

Introduction

APRIL 1942

Standing on the shore along a desolate strip of beach, a group of fishermen huddle in the darkness and watch the distant flames from a burning ship. They decide to venture out in their fishing dory and try to save anyone who might have survived this inferno. It is the time of World War II and ships are being torpedoed and sunk off the North Carolina coast.

Pushing their small wooden boat into the surf, the men row eastward for several hours toward the still-burning ship. It is near midnight as the men pull hard through the calm seas. The unmistakable whine of diesel engines breaks the silence. Suddenly, cutting through the darkness, a powerful beam of bright light illuminates the dory. The fishermen are startled and nearly blinded. The rumble of the diesels intensifies as the light draws nearer, and then moves away from the rescue boat. A surfaced German submarine will let the rescuers live. The frightened but grateful men turn the boat around and row back to shore.

My grandfather told this true story to me half a century ago. It happened off the coast of Kitty Hawk Beach in the spring of 1942. The burning ship was probably the *Byron D. Benson* and the U-boat possibly the U-552 commanded by Corvette Captain Eric Topp. Topp who on October 31, 1941 sank the *U.S.S. Reuben James*, also torpedoed and sank the *Benson* five months later on April 5.

A few minutes after midnight on April 14, 1942, another German U-boat running on the surface less than 15 miles from the North Carolina coastline was overhauled and sunk by an American destroyer. The submarine was the U-85 and the destroyer the *U. S. S. Roper*. The entire crew on the U-boat died; all on the *Roper* survived. After a lightning battle that lasted less than one hour, the first German U-boat engaged on the surface by a U. S. Navy warship after America's entry into the Second World War had been defeated and was on the bottom.

This is the story of that U-boat, her captain and crew, and the diving and adventure that have followed. From U-85's beginning at Flender Werft Shipyard in Lubeck Germany, to her end on the floor of the Atlantic 15 miles northeast of Oregon Inlet North Carolina, this U-boat has been a source of mystery and exploration for divers and historians over the past half century. You can find her today on the sandy ocean floor, a shadow in the sea, rusting away in the saltwater where she sank stern-first that early April morning in 1942.

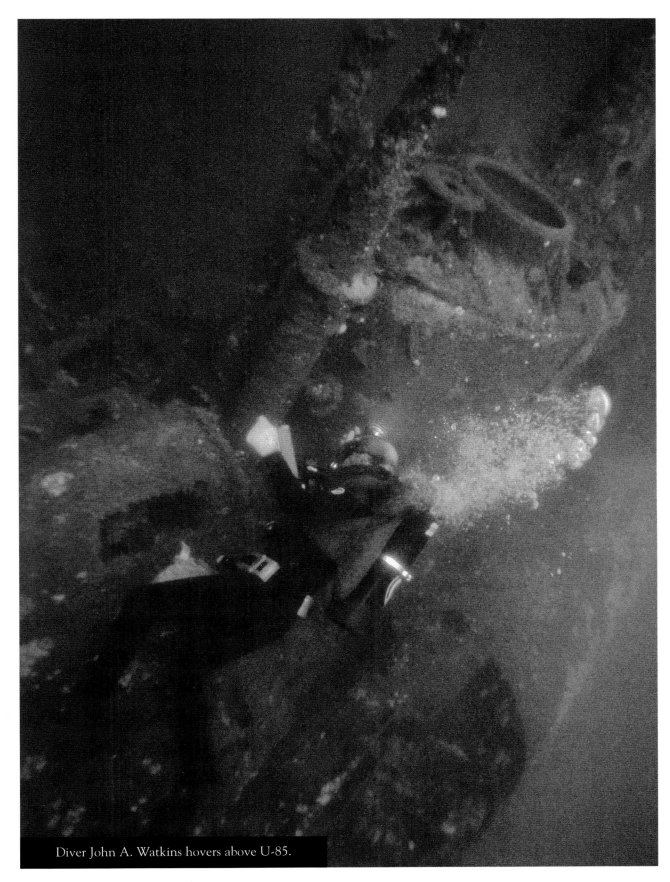

Diver John A. Watkins hovers above U-85.

The Adventure Begins

Kitty Hawk

Life at the beach began for me in June 1943 when I spent my first summer at Kitty Hawk. My grandfather built several oceanfront cottages there in the 1930s for our family to enjoy during the summer months. I'm told that our closest neighbor was at least half a mile away. U-85 was already history and lying on the bottom less than 20 miles from my summer home.

Kitty Hawk was different then. There were only a few scattered cottages along the oceanfront. America had been involved in the Second World War for more than a year and German U-boats were operating along the coastline. Debris from sea battles that occurred within miles of our cottages often washed ashore.

Mom took me in the ocean before I could walk. I learned how to use a mask and fins before 1950. I was too young to realize it then, but the sea and its treasury of sunken ships was right behind our cottages.

Scuba

My first scuba tank, regulator, and weight belt were purchased from a grocery store. The store, Andersons, owned by colorful Outer Banks character William James "Wild Bill" Anderson, was where I worked in the summertime. Bill was the deputy sheriff, justice of the peace, real estate broker, mayor, reverend, and almost anything else you could imagine. He could arrest you, try you, find you guilty or innocent, and even marry you if that's what you wanted. He could drink more, talk more, tell bigger tales and play more than anyone on the beach. He was a good friend to have if you needed something. Bill gave me a job packing groceries for the summer shoppers when I was ten.

I discovered the diving gear in one of Bill's sporting goods catalogues. Bill ordered two sets, one for me and one for a friend of mine, Walt Spcence.

Jim Bunch

10

My order included an Aquamaster double hose regulator, a weight belt with 10 pounds of weights, and a steel 72 cubic foot tank with a K-valve. All of the equipment was made by U. S. Divers Company. I already owned a Diver's Champion mask, a snorkel, a spear gun, and a pair of Voit Viking fins.

I decided to try out my new equipment at *Perry's* shipwreck. This mysterious place in the ocean that seemed to turn the water purple was named in honor of Perry's Drive-In. *Perry's* was the favorite spot to dine in those days and was located on the beach road across the street from the ocean. On the shallow bottom at *Perry's*, the twisted remains of two large ships that grounded within 100 feet of each other in the 1920s provided a gathering place for marine life and the few local skin-divers.

Today, this wreck site is called the *Triangle* and is still a popular beach dive for shallow water adventures. It can be found just off the beach at 2nd Street in Kill Devil Hills. Perry's Drive-In is now Goombays. The two ships are the *Carl Gerhard* and the *Kyzickes*.

I took the scuba class on the way to Perry's wreck. A friend, Norwood Rector, had experience using scuba and was willing to instruct me in the basics of compressed air diving. Since I was to young to drive, Norwood picked me up at my cottage and we headed down the beach road toward *Perry's*. Norwood was a retired UDT diver and was married to Mr. Perry's daughter Carol. He also owned a small dive shop, the first one on the Outer Banks, located in the garage behind the Drive In. The garage walls were filled with U. S. Divers Company posters and banners. The company's owner and inventor of the aqualung, Jacques Cousteau, was our diving hero.

Author's Son Mike and Jacques Cousteau aboard Cousteau's R/V *Calypso*.

The class lasted about five minutes. "Just don't hold your breath," Norwood said "and you'll be alright." Since there were no organized certification classes in the mid-fifties, this seemed good enough. I passed the class by answering, "OK."

We carried our equipment across the sand dunes onto the beach in front of *Perry's* wreck. It wasn't difficult since all we each had was a tank, regulator, weight belt, mask, and fins.

In those days, there was no such thing as a buoyancy compensator, octopus, or pressure gauge. We didn't even have a backpack for the tanks, only nylon straps attached directly to them. We pushed a rubber raft in front of us for buoyancy.

After gearing up, we swam to the spot about 200 yards out where the surface water looked purple and descended. Having the means to breathe underwater and stay as long as I wanted was the beginning of many future visits to the world of sunken shipwrecks.

A diver explores the *Triangle* Wrecks.

U-85 Fever

I heard about the U-85 in the mid 1970s. My first experience there was in July 1978. The only boat visiting the wreck then was a 24-foot speedboat sometimes dive-boat owned by Captain Jim Stuart. The boat, a FishNautique, and Stuart knew only one speed, wide-open.

Captain Jim Stuart heads for U-85 On his D/V *Sea Fox*. Courtesy Sandy Sanderson

Stuart had been introduced to the 85 by Larry Keen in 1977 and was already obsessed with exploring the submarine. Keen, who had led trips there for several summers, would also return to the wreck many times in the coming years.

No matter what the condition of the sea, Jim didn't believe in wasting time getting to the submarine. Once the boat left the dock, it was every man for himself. After a fast ride out, covering the 25 miles to the site in about 35 minutes, we were all in the water, down the line, and swimming along the deck of the U-85.

The wreck was much more intact in the 70s than it is today. My first view of it was spectacular. Visibility was near 50 feet and the unmistakable cigar shape of a submarine sent shivers through my already cold skin. The deck faring was still attached to the pressure hull with many storage compartments evident. Rounds for the 88mm. gun were scattered all over the deck and the two storage containers on top of the pressure hull with torpedoes inside were easy to identify. The periscopes and hatch covers were also still in place. All the air intake and exhaust truncking could be seen resting on the pressure hull. The wooden decking and bridge faring around the conning tower were already gone. The wreck was loaded with fish that circled us during the entire dive.

When the dive ended and we headed for shore at 50 miles an hour, a feeling of exhilaration and pride swept over me. I had visited a shipwreck that very few had seen. I knew then like my friend Stuart, I would be back.

John A. Watkins shines his light into a hole Through U-85's pressure hull created by *Roper's* three-inch shell. 1978.

German Type VIIB Submarine
24 constructed between 1936 and 1940

U-boat	Builder	Work #	Built
U-45 - U-50	Germaniawerft AG, Kiel	580-585	1936-1937
U-51 - U-55	Germaniawerft AG, Kiel	586-590	1938-1939
U-73 U-76	Vegesacker Werft, Vegesack	1-4	1938-1940
U-83 U-87	Flender-Werke AG, Lubeck	291, 280-283	1938-1941
U-99 U-102	Germaniawerft AG, Kiel	593-596	1937-1940

Technical Specifications

Displacement: (tons)	704 (d) 753 (sf) 857 (sm) 1040 (total)	Speed: (knots)	17.9 (sf) 8.0 (sm)
Length: (m)	66.5 oa 48.8 ph	Range (miles/knots)	8700/10 (sf) 90/4 (sm)
Beam: (m)	6.2 oa 4.7ph	Torpedoes:	14
		Mines:	39 TMB
Draught: (m)	4.75	Deck Gun:	8.8cm C35L/45 220 rounds
Height: (m)	9.5	AA Gun	2cm C30
Power: (hp)	3200 (sf) 750 (sm)	Crew	44-48 men
		Max. Depth:	725 feet

sm = submerged, sf = surfaced oa = overall

ph = pressure hull, hp = horsepower

The Boat

At the beginning of World War II, Germany had fewer than 30 operational U-boats in service. The conceptual uses for these boats ranged from mine laying and reconnaissance to an all out war on shipping. The larger boats of the IXC class were preferred by the Naval leadership as strategic weapons, while the smaller and more maneuverable Class VII boats were used to wage the convoy battles of the North Atlantic.

All of these submarines were essentially surface craft with the capability of staying submerged only for very short periods of time. They all relied on diesel engines for surface propulsion and electric motors for running submerged. The electric motors were powered by storage batteries carried below the submarine's flooring. These batteries required daily recharging by the diesel engines and could only be done when the U-boat was surfaced.

Type VIIB

U-85, a member of the second generation of Class Type VII U-boats was one of 24 submarines built and designated by design characteristics as a Type VIIB. The Type VII boat, of which 709 were built by Germany between 1936 and 1945, was the workhorse of the *Kriegsmarine* undersea fleet during the Second World War. The majority of Type VII boats were classed as Type VIIC's and included 660 submarines. Of the 1152 U-boats built by Germany between 1935 and 1945, the majority were Type VII's.

The Type VIIB, out-classing its VIIA predecessor with improved speed, range, and weaponry, became in early 1938 the preferred operational U-boat of the Commander-and-Chief of submarines BdU Karl Donitz. Had it not been for several technical developments in sensor equipment and the need for more hull space, the VIIB would have been Germany's most-produced U-boat of the war.

The first Type VIIB, U-45, was commissioned June 25, 1938, and the last one, U-87, August 19, 1941. Of the VIIB boats, U-45 to U-55 and U-99 to U-102 were built at the Germania Shipyards in Kiel, U-73 to U-76 at Bremer Vulcan in Vegesack, and U-83 to U-87 at Flender Werft in Lubeck. Type VIIB's included Otto Kretschmer's famous U-99, Gunther Prien's U-47, Schepke's U-100, and Bleichrodt's U-48, the most successful U-boat of the war sinking 53 ships. By 1945, only the U-46, U-48, U-52 and U-78 were still afloat. Their own crews scuttled them that year. At war's end, the entire group of 24 VIIB's had sunk more than 250 ships.

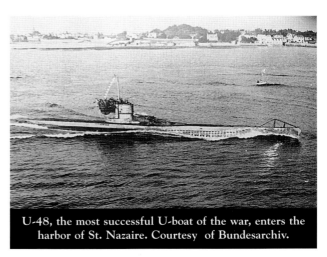

U-48, the most successful U-boat of the war, enters the harbor of St. Nazaire. Courtesy of Bundesarchiv.

U-85

The "K" Office of The *Oberkommando der Kriegsmarine* contracted U-85 and 7 other VIIB's on June 9, 1938. The order number was 291, 280-283, and the building yard chosen was Flender-Werke AG. The keel was laid December 18, 1939 and the boat launched April 10, 1941. Commissioning by *Oberleutnant* Eberhard Greger took place on June 7, 1941. The boat was given a Feldpost number of M40935. Every German naval unit had its own Feldpost number. This number, used primarily as a postal address, was also used as a security device to recall a U-boat crew from a public place.

Conning tower pressure hull of a type V11 U-boat ready for assembly. Courtesy Bundesarchiv.

U-85 was a single-hull design, the pressure hull also being the outer hull. The hull was fabricated from steel, ranged in thickness from .75 in. to .65 in. and was reinforced with strengthening ribs every 24 inches. It's weakest point was where the conning tower was attached and was .88 in. thick here.

The pressure hull was fabricated from 8 steel modules that were built separately and welded together. A large hole in the top of module five, located next to the aftermost module, was left open as an access point to outfit and equip the submarine.

After all items, including the diesel engines and electric motors were loaded inside, module five was sealed and the conning tower pressure hull welded in place. The superstructure, extending from the bow to the stern, was now welded on. The saddle tanks and deck armaments were added last.

When completed, U-85 was 218 feet long and had a 160-foot pressure hull. It had a 20-foot beam, a keel-to-bridge height of 31 feet, and a 15.5-foot draft. The boat displaced 753 tons with the fuel and water tanks full and 1040 tons fully loaded and submerged. Two diesels with superchargers provided surface power of 3200 horsepower and a maximum speed of 20 mph. Two electric motors produced 750 horsepower and a submerged running speed of 10 mph. The two propulsion systems together enabled U-85 to travel 10,000 miles without refueling.

U-85 was armed with four bow and one stern torpedo tubes. As an improvement over the original Type VII, the stern tube was relocated within the casing and was reloadable from the aft torpedo compartment. The boat's two rudders, an upgrade from the single rudder found on Type VIIs, allowed torpedoes fired from the stern tube to pass between them. Additional storage outside the pressure hull and under the stern torpedo compartment flooring made it possible to increase the torpedo load from 11 to 14. One 88mm. C35 L/45 gun fitted forward of the conning tower and one 20mm. C30 flak gun aft of the tower gave U-85 the weaponry to fight on and below the surface.

Inside the pressure hull, above the flooring, the boat had the following compartments: forward torpedo room and crews quarters, officer and chief rates quarters, control room with attack center (conning tower) above, senior rates quarters and galley, diesel room, electric motor room and after-torpedo compartment.

The forward torpedo room was 36 feet long and had space for 10 torpedoes, 12 bunks, and 24 enlisted men. The officer and chief rates quarters were aft of the forward torpedo room and accommodated five officers including the Captain and four chief petty officers. This space was 24 feet long and separated from the forward area by a thin metal wall and rectangular doorway. The radio and sound rooms were located on the starboard side of this compartment adjacent to the control room. Next came the 20-foot long control room, accessible on both ends by round watertight hatches. Above the control room, another watertight round hatch led to the attack center. Behind the control room, the senior rates quarters and galley consumed another 22 feet of pressure hull and included 8 bunks and room for 16 men to eat and sleep. The 24-foot diesel engine room with its narrow hallway between the two MAN diesel engines came next, located behind a thin metal wall and a rectangular door. The aft-room on U-85 was the electric motor and stern torpedo room. This 34-foot long room held the two electric motors for submerged running and the stern torpedo tube. No men slept in this compartment.

The area below the deck plating of the officers quarters, senior rates quarters, and control room was almost as large as the living and working space above. Here were found the battery rooms and the 125 batteries, the 256 cubic foot magazine, fuel and fresh water tanks, main div-

ing tanks, and the S-Gerat (sound detection equipment) compartment. The forward trim tank, torpedo compensating tanks, and storage space for four reserve torpedoes were below the forward torpedo room and crew's quarters. The aft trim tank, torpedo compensating tank, and storage space for 1 torpedo were found below the stern torpedo loading compartment.

U-85 docks at St. Nazaire behind the U-751 Feb. 23, 1942. Courtesy of The Bundesarchiv

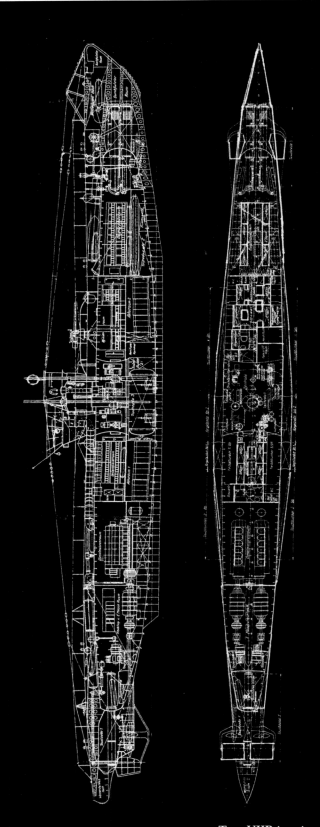

Type VIIB interior profile and working floor plan.

The Crew

All U-boat men were supposedly volunteers but this was not always the case. Any person judged fit for U-boat service was required to volunteer for it. Forty-six men made up the crew of U-85. Whether they were all volunteers is unknown. They did range in age from 19 to 36 and were divided by rank and number into three groups composed of officers, non-commissioned officers, and enlisted men. The non-commissioned officers were warrant, chief petty and petty officers. Each man except for the officers functioned as either a seaman or a member of the technical division. The night U-85 was sunk, there were five officers, six senior non-commissioned officers, eleven petty officers and 24 enlisted men on board. This

Oberleutnant Zur See **Eberhard Greger.**
Courtesy of the Bundesarchiv.

group of men was the LAST crew but NOT the starting crew from 1941. Many of the original crew members had gone on to other assignments, mostly after the third cruise.

Officers

The commanding officer on U-85 was her Captain, *Oberleutnant zur See* Eberhard Greger. Greger, a member of Crew 35, was 27 years old and a graduate of the Marineschule Murwik in Flensburg where he was commissioned an *Oberleutnant zur See* on October 1, 1939. Unlike their Annapolis counterparts, German Naval Officers were designated by the year they entered the naval academy rather than when they graduated. Forty-five U-boat commanders emerged from the Crew of 1935.

Before taking command of U-85, Greger had gained experience as the second watch officer aboard the destroyer *Wolfgang Zenker* and the first watch officer under the command of Fritz Julius Lemp aboard the famous U-30 and U-110. Lemp mistakenly sank the passenger liner *Athenia* several days after the beginning of The Second World War and on May 9, 1941 allowed the U-110 and her three-rotor *enigma machine* to be captured on the surface. On the morning of the 10th, U-110 sank while under tow by the *HMS Bulldog*. Greger commissioned and commanded the 85 from her launching on June 7, 1941 until she was sunk in April of 1942.

With two years of combat experience behind him, *Oberleutnant* Greger was an able commanding officer with a seasoned crew. On him, as with all U-boat commanders, was placed the ultimate responsibility for the U-boat's success or failure. Of his many duties, one was to supervise the First Watch Officer during surface torpedo attacks. Having been the IWO on the U-30 and the U-110, he was very experienced in surface engagements and responsible for several sinkings. He was probably on the bridge doing this the night U-85 was sunk by the *Roper*.

As Kommandant, he had his own private quarters adjacent to the control room. The radio and sound rooms were only a few feet from his bunk. He spent most of his time in the control room, on the bridge, or in the conning tower behind the attack periscope.

Greger and *Obersteuermann* Heinz Wendt bring U-85 alongside the dock at St. Nazaire. Courtesy of the Bundesarchiv.

Four other officers, *Oberleutnant zur See* Kurt Fraesdorff, *Oberleutnant* Helmut Lechler, *Oberleutnant* Ingenieur Hans Sanger and *Leutnant zur See* Wolfgang Komorowski were the other senior officers on board the U-85 and had various responsibilities. Their bunks were in the compartment adjacent to the Captain's quarters and just forward of the sound room. A permanent mess table here was used by the four officers and the Captain as a wardroom and discussion center.

24-year-old *Oberleutnant zur See* Helmut Lechler, the first watch officer or IWO, was the second most important man on the boat and took command in the event that something incapacitated the Captain. He was responsible for the readiness of the boat's torpedoes and conducted surface torpedo attacks. He also supervised and organized the first bridge watch. He probably fired the one torpedo that barely missed the *Roper*.

The second watch officer, 24-year-old *Leutnant zur See* Wolfgang Komorowski, had responsibility for the U-boat's deck guns, provisions, and communications systems. He was in charge of the *enigma* machine and encrypted secret radio messages when necessary. The second bridge watch was his responsibility. On April 14, he was busy directing the planned use of

U-85's 88mm. deck gun and 20mm. flak gun against the *Roper*.

25 year-old *Oberleutnant zur See* Hans Sanger, the chief engineer or L. I., was responsible for the technical operation of U-85. All physical systems on the boat fell under his control. He kept the Captain advised on all technical matters effecting the boat. He was, in many respects, another Captain. Most of his time was spent in the control room working with the Captain. He had no specific watch but was on constant call. He maintained the diving data log and his own war diary for the operation of the vessel's engines. He was probably at his station behind the two planesmen in the control room during the battle of April 14. He eventually abandoned ship and was the only officer recovered from the sea by the *Roper*.

Oberleutnant Zur See Hans Sanger. Sanger was the L.I., or chief engineer on U-85. Courtesy of Ed Caram.

The fourth officer, 27-year-old *Oberleutnant zur See* Kurt Fraesdorff, was a commander-in-training. He was on board to observe an operational U-boat and learn what he could from her officers and men. He would probably have been promoted to a U-boat commander before his next patrol.

Crew members are greeted by KK Sohler, Chief of the 7th U-boat Flotilla after docking at St. Nazaire on Feb. 23, 1942. Courtesy of the Bundesarchiv.

Crew members of U-85 engaged in the docking process. The boat had just returned from War Cruise three. Courtesy of the Bundesarchiv

Greger talks with KL Bigalk, Captain of U-751 and KK Sohler, Chief
of the 7th U-boat flotilla on the docks at St. Nazaire.

Chief Petty Officers

The six chief petty officers had responsibilities almost equal to those of the senior officers. The four most senior of these men shared a compartment aft of the bow torpedo room and adjacent to the officers quarters. They ate and slept here but spent most of their time in different areas of the boat.

Most senior of these was *Obersteuermann* Heinz Wendt. Wendt, the 28-year-old chief helmsman and navigator was responsible for navigational and provisional matters aboard the U-boat. He had direct authority over the boat's helmsman and was in charge of plotting and recording the boat's course. Wendt also acted as third watch officer.

The next senior CPO was 25-year-old *Oberbootsmannsmaat* Oskar Prantl. Also referred to as Number One, he was responsible for the conduct of the seamans division of the crew. It was his job to see that each man's clothing and equipment was in order. He also tried to settle disputes among the seamen before the problems reached the Captain. He also was responsible for the cleaning of the vessel and the fourth watch. Prantl was probably with the Captain on the bridge of the conning tower entering data into the torpedo attack calculator just before the U-85 went down.

All ammunition and small arms stored aboard the U-boat were accountable to Prantl's first mate, *Bootsmannsmaat* Helmut Kaiser. Referred to as Number Two, Kaiser was required to sign off for all of the above items when checked out or used by the crew. Prantl's third mate, *Bootsmannsmaat* Willy Matthies was responsible for the final cleanup of the boat when it returned to port.

The two remaining senior CPOs, *Stabsobermaschinist* Eugen Ungethuem, and *Obermaschinist* Heinrich Adrian were responsible for the diesel engines and electric motors that powered the submarine. They reported directly to the L. I. Hans Sanger. They also had responsibility for supervision of the technical division of the crew. CPO *Obermaschinist* Fredrich Strobel served under these two men.

The last CPO, *Oberfunkmaat* Martin Wittmann, was responsible for the radio and sound rooms and the sending and receiving of messages around the clock. The *enigma* machine and its operation were under his care. Petty Officer, *Funkmaat* Konstant Weidmann, and enlisted men *Funkobergefreiter* Hans Wobst and *Funkgefreiter* Heinz Waschmann paired together with Wittmann to carry out the 6 four-hour watch periods every 24 hours. These four men also had the more pleasant duty of playing the boat's collection of phonograph records.

Petty officers And Enlisted Men

Eleven petty officers and 24 enlisted men made up this group. They comprised the technical and seaman's divisions and did most of the work on the boat. The technical group included the torpedo men, motormen, electricians, radiomen and dieselmen. The men classified as seamen were stewards, laborers, watchmen, and the cook.

The petty officers lived in the compartment aft of the control room, the enlisted men in the forward torpedo room. One petty officer, the leading torpedoman *Mechanikermatt* Oskar Hansen, slept in the forward torpedo room, keeping a close maintenance check on the torpedoes.

The entire complement was lost as a result of the battle that took place on April 14, 1942.

Machine-gun fire and the onboard explosion of one 3-inch shell killed some. After abandoning ship most died in the water from internal injuries caused by exploding depth charges dropped by the *Roper*.

Before this battle, no casualties had occurred aboard the U-85 since her commissioning the previous June. 29 bodies were recovered from the sea and buried at Hampton National Cemetery. The other 17 men, including the Commandant Eberhard Greger, were presumed lost.

Baubelehrung

The Captain and members of U-85's crew gathered at Flender Werft Shipyard as the submarine entered the last stages of construction. This meeting of the 45 men who would work and live together on the U-boat was *Baubelehrung,* or the construction acquaintance process. This process made sure that all crewmembers knew every possible detail about the U-boat and each other. Each man was expected to know not only the intricate details of the boat's construction, but

Oberbootsman Oskar Prantl. Courtesy Richard A. Hall

also how to perform most of the tasks of the other crewmen. The crew and the boat were brought together into a single unit greater than the sum of all the parts, mechanical and human. U85's *Baubelehrung* ended June 7, 1941 when the boat was commissioned into the *Kriegsmarine*.

Greger and Sohler talk with U-85's officers on the deck of U-85 following the boat's return from her third war cruise. Courtesy of the Bundesarchiv.

CREW OF U-85 April 14, 1942

5	OFFICERS:	Oberleutnant zur See Ebehard Greger	CAPTAIN
		Oberleutnant zur See Helmut Lechler	IWO
		Leutnant zur See Wolfgang Komorowski	2WO
		Oberleutnant zur See Hans Sanger	LI
		Oberleutnant zur See Kurt Fraesdorff	CIT

6	CHIEF PETTY OFFICERS:	Obersteuermann Heinz Wendt	HELMSMAN
		Oberboatsman Oskar Prantl	BOATSWAIN
		Obermaschinist Heinrick Adrian	E. ENGINE
		Stabsobermaschinist Eugene Ungethuen	DIESEL ENGINE
		Obermaschinist Martin Wittmann	
		Obermachinist Friedrick Strobel	

11 PETTY OFFICERS

Mt Konstant Weidmann	Mt Herbert Waack	Mt Heinrick Rogge
Mt Arthur Piotrowski	Mt Willy Matthies	Mt Helmut Kaiser
Mt Herbert Heller	Mt Oskar Hansen	Mt Herbert Albig
Mtr Walter Kiefer	Mt Herbert Peemoller	

24 ENLISTED MEN

Obergefreiter

Hans Wobst	Gerh Wagner	Werner Schumacher
Fritz Roder	Jon Letiz	Ernst Kuckelhaus
Jon Killermann	Walter Gunzl	Albert Frey
Fritz Behla		

Gefreiter

Heinz Waschmann	Horst Spodding	Karl Schultes
Gunter Schulz	Joachin Schultz	Eric Schorisch
Gustav Schon	Werner Schneider	Willy Metge
Jos Kleibrink	Otto Hagenmaer	Eric Degenkolb
Wilhelm Brinkmann	Gerhard Ammann	

45 TOTAL

Crew members at home and aboard U-85. These pictures were recovered from the crewmen after the sinking. Courtesy of the National Archives.

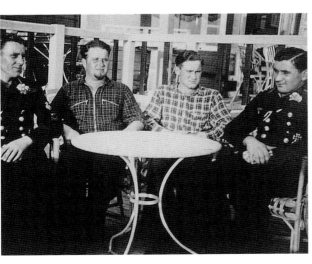

U-85 Goes To War

U-85 officially entered the service of the *Kreigsmarine* on June 7, 1941 when her Captain, *Oberleutenant* Eberhard Greger, commissioned her. Next, hull and engine trials at Kiel under the U-Boat Acceptance Command and handling trials under the Technical Training Group for front line U-boats consumed most of the summer months of 1941. Finally tactical convoy and attack exercises conducted off Pillau in the Baltic were successfully completed and the boat was declared FRONTREIF fit to sail on operational patrols.

Additional information about U-85's activities during the summer of 1941 is revealed in a diary kept by *stabsobermaschinist* Eugen Ungethum. The diary was found floating in the water near the spot where U-85 went down. In his diary, Ungethum records that on July 26th the U-85 got underway for Norway, possibly from Lubeck at 5 in the morning. On the following day and 22 hours later, the boat tied up alongside the Blucher Bridge at Horton, Oslofjord. From Sunday 27 July until Wednesday, the 6th of August, the boat remained at Horton. Liberty was granted to part of her crew on July 30th and 31st to visit Oslo.

She left Horton on August 6th at six in the afternoon in a convoy for Trondheim by way of Christiansen, Scavenger, Moldjne and Aalesund. Arriving in Lofjord on August 10th, she tied up alongside the *Hertha*, a depot ship for submarines.

From Monday, 11 August to Thursday, 28 August, U-85 held firing practice in Trodheimfjord. On the morning of August 13th she was rammed in 45 feet of water by the small destroyer *T-151* damaging her number one diving tank and the steering gear.

U-85 was painted, given a final overhaul in dry-dock and assigned to the 3rd U-boat flotilla as a front boat on September 1, 1941. An emblem - a wild boar - emulating her Captain Eberhard Greger, was painted on her conning tower. The German translation of boar is "Eber" meaning strong like a boar.

According to Wolfgang Klaue, Lothar-Guenther Buchheim, then a marine painter and who later wrote the story of Wolfgang Peterson's film *Das Boot* painted the picture on the tower during the summer of 1941. A rose was added to the emblem in the fall when the hometown of Captain Greger became the sponsor of U-85. Greger's hometown was Lieberose meaning "love rose."

Lothar-Guenther Bucheim paints a wild boar on the Conning tower of U-85. Courtesy Wolfgang Klaue.

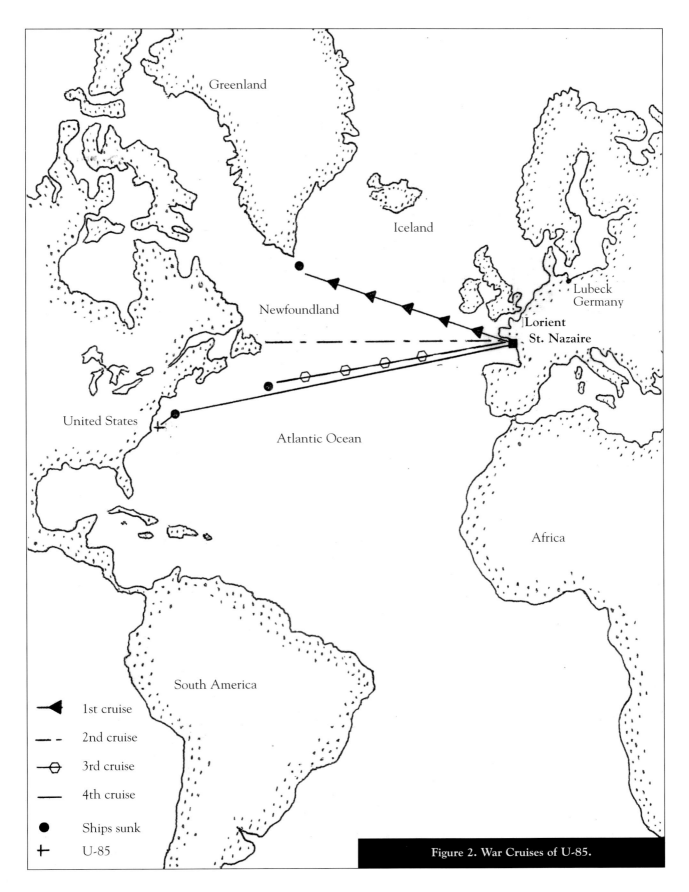

Greenland

Iceland

Lubeck
Germany

Newfoundland

Lorient
St. Nazaire

United States

Atlantic Ocean

Africa

South America

◄ 1st cruise

– – 2nd cruise

⬡ 3rd cruise

— 4th cruise

● Ships sunk

+ U-85

Figure 2. War Cruises of U-85.

U-85 arrives in St. Nazaire Feb. 23, 1942 following her 3rd war cruise. Note the two victory pennants on the flag pole behind Obersteurmann Wendt. Greger mistakenly thought he had sunk the 9000-ton merchantman *Port Wyndham*. He did sink the *Empire Fusselier* indicated by the 6000 ton pennant. Bundesarchiv.

First War Cruise

U-85 slipped her moorings at the Port of Trondheim Norway on the night of August 28th, 1941. Running on the surface north of the North Sea and into the North Atlantic, the new untested U-boat and crew would encounter action almost immediately.

On the first day out, British aircraft patrolling the area forced the U-boat to submerge. On the 3rd day a freighter was sighted by U-85's lookouts in the northern North Sea but escaped by turning and running away. The next day, another steamer was spotted. U-85, looking for an early victory, submerged and moved into attack position. The ship was judged too small to waste a torpedo on and the attack was broken off. Greger continued his patrol toward the west.

On September 2nd, the 6th day of the cruise, a plane spotted U-85 on the surface and dropped three bombs before U-85 could submerge. Later in the day, U-105 was sighted and the 2 boats exchanged messages and experiences for a short period.

By the 4th of September, the boat moved south of the Denmark Straits and took up a position with 13 other submarines along a line southwest of Iceland. This group of U-boats designated group MARKGRAF by BdU Karl Donitz hoped to locate and sink convoyed ships heading to and from the British Isles.

The presence of the MARKGRAF group was known to British intelligence and some of the con-voys were re-routed to avoid it. Numerous Allied aircraft circled the patrol area and sent U-85 diving for cover several times on the 4th and 5th of September.

With their own information from B-dienst, U-Boat Command shifted the entire MARKFRAF group 175 miles west on the 6th of September. The 14 U-boats quickly reformed their line southwest of Greenland.

On the morning of September 9, U-85 and U-81 were patrolling along the ice pack near the east coast of Greenland when Greger ran into a huge mass of ships near Cape Farewell. Around seven oclock, U-85's lookouts heard detonations and saw a glow northwest of their position. By ten they could see the smoke from the ships.

Greger had found slow convoy 42. It was composed of 65 vessels and was making about five knots. The Canadian destroyer *Skeena* and 3 corvettes were the groups escorts. This information was quickly radioed to U-boat Headquarters and BdU Admiral Karl Donitz.

Acting on U-85's contact report, the entire MARKGRAF group was ordered to close and attack. Three boats, U-82, U-432, and U-652 immediately joined U-85 on the 9th. Greger and his crew were about to begin their most intense battle of the war.

It began with a general alarm when U-85's lookouts spotted Allied aircraft around noon. The U-boat submerged and closed for an underwater attack on the slow moving convoy. Five torpedoes were fired at close range but no detonations followed.

Defective torpedoes either missed or bounced off the ships without exploding.

U-85 surfaced and immediately spotted two steamers. The nearer one appeared to be a lookout vessel and the other was motionless in the water. Greger submerged and moved away, fearing a submarine trap. One hour later the U-boat surfaced and continued following the convoy through drifting icebergs.

U-85's pursuit of the convoy continued into the 10th of September. Still off the east coast of Greenland and near the large group of ships, U-85 was spotted by a destroyer. The destroyer opened fire and U-85 immediately submerged. A depth charge followed U-85 down where she remained for over an hour.

Surfacing later Greger maneuvered into a position ahead of the convoy and again submerged. As the ships approached in the late afternoon, Greger fired a spread of two torpedoes at a 7,000-ton vessel, hitting the target. Thirty minutes later he fired two more torpedoes at two 5000-ton ships and recorded two hits. Only one of the three ships, the 4,700-ton SS *Thistleglen* went to the bottom. The other two were damaged and made it to port.

Submerging immediately U-85 was pounced on by the destroyer *Skeena*. The extensive depth charging that followed sent the U-boat diving to 308 feet and created havoc within the submarine. Extensive damage, much of which was unrepairable, resulted from exploding depth charges. Two hours later Greger attempted to surface three times, each time being forced to dive immediately because of the presence of aircraft dropping bombs.

Three more hours passed before U-85 was able to surface and try to repair the damage she had sus-

tained during the 35-hour pursuit. A test dive during the morning of the 11th showed the boat to be in a state of limited readiness to submerge. Unable to continue the patrol, Greger set course for St. Nazaire and home.

The convoy battle ended on the 14th of September after 16 ships had been sunk by the U-boats. Two German submarines, U-207 and U-501, were also sunk. After 22 days at sea, U-85 arrived at her new base of St. Nazaire on the French coast September 18, 1941.

Second War Cruise

U-85 left St. Nazaire on the afternoon of 16 October and headed for the western North Atlantic to join nine other U-boats forming group SCHLAGETOT.

On the 4th day out Horst Uphoffic in U-84 ran into a group of large ships 400 miles west of Ireland. One destroyer and two cutters escorted the five big merchant ships. They were moving east at 14 knots in the direction of the British Isles.

Doubtful that the SCHLAGETOT group could reach these ships before a canopy of allied aircraft would be sent to cover them, Donitz instructed the other U-boats of the group not to pursue without a good chance of success.

On the 20th Donitz canceled the operation and ordered all the SCHLAGETOT boats to move northwest toward Greenland. One boat, Reinhard Hardegan in U-123, disregarded the order and continued east toward the merchant ships. He closed the convoy in the early morning hours of the 21st, maneuvered through the escorts, and fired his bow torpedoes. His target was the 14,000-ton Curnard White Star Liner *Aurania*. One torpedo struck the ship but did not sink her. Hardegan believing that the *Aurania* was on the bottom, got off a contact report to Donitz and was mistakenly credited with a sinking.

U-123 reversed course and again headed for Greenland. Around noon, the bridge watch spotted smoke on the horizon. It was inbound convoy SL 89 composed of 20 freighters and tankers. Hardegan sent another contact report and Donitz again ordered U-85 and group SCHLAGETOT to reverse course, find, and attack the large convoy.

Two U-boats found the convoy on the night of October 21st and Siegfried Rollmann in U-82 sank two British freighters. U-85, chasing the convoy in heavy seas and low visibility, was informed by German air reconnaissance aircraft that the group of ships was about 40 miles away. The seas were so rough that waves were breaking over U-85's bridge and seawater poured into the control room through the open conning tower hatch. Unable to see in the blinding rain, the bridge watch was useless and the U-boat had to reduce speed. To make things worse, a four motor American long-range bomber dropped six depth charges barely missing the boat. Even if Greger could have found the convoy, the sea was too rough to launch torpedoes.

Finally arriving in the operations area on the 23rd of October U-85 was met by a sea of British escorts patrolling behind the distant convoy. The operation was again called off by U-Boat Command on the 24th and the group ordered again to the coast of Greenland.

On October 28, U-85 and the other boats of the SCHLAGETOT group formed a 150-mile line about 350 miles south of the Greenland coast. One day later, slow convoy 52 left Sydney, Nova Scotia. The convoy was composed of 36 ships and had 9 Canadian escorts. The ships sailed directly into the path of Unno von Fischels U-374. Fischel was a member of group MORDBRENNER operating south of group SCHLAGETOT.

U-374's contact report went out on November 1 and all the SCHLAGETOT boats, now operating as group RAUBRITTER, raced south to intercept the convoy. Hans Heinz in U-202 sank two ships and Hans Peter Hinsch in U-569 sank one. Rolf Mutzelburg in U-203 sank two more that same day. U-85 and most of the other boats were unable to find the convoy because of heavy fog.

Fearing additional loses, the Admiralty ordered the remaining Allied ships to abort and return to Nova Scotia. The U-boats lost contact on the 5th.

The RAUBRITTER boats, low on fuel, began their trip home on the 15th of November. On the 19th, U-85, U-133, U-571, and U-577 formed patrol line STORTEBECKER in search of convoy OG 77. The convoy was not found and the group was ordered to return to France.

On November 27, 1941, after 47 days at sea, U-85 returned to Lorient low on fuel and with a full load of torpedoes.

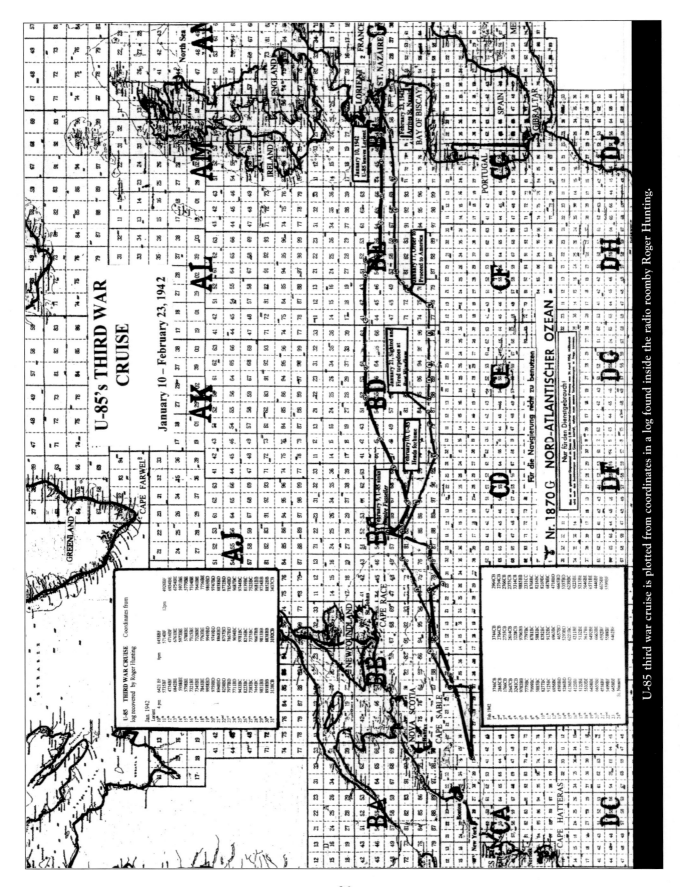

U-85 third war cruise is plotted from coordinates in a log found inside the radio room by Roger Hunting.

36

Germany Declares War

Germany declared war on the United States December 11, 1941, fourteen days after U-85 returned to Lorient from her 2nd patrol. Operation PAUKENSCHLAG began December 18th when 6 Type 1X U-boats were sent westward by Admiral Karl Donitz to sink American shipping along the East Coast of the United States. Ten Type Vlls followed later that month. U-85 would be one of the 26 German submarines sent to the Americas in January.

Third War Cruise

U-85 left Lorient January 10th on a course for Gibraltar and the Mediterranean. Clearing the Bay of Biscay, U-85 sailed west for six days, turning southwest on the 15th into 6-foot seas and light southwesterly winds.

On the 17th a new operational order was received from U-Boat Headquarters directing U-85 to change course and proceed to American waters.

On the 18th and about 300 miles at sea, U-85 turned due west. The wind and seas were light and the U-boat moved cautiously on the surface toward the American coast.

On the 21st of January and U-85's 11th day at sea, Greger sighted a lone ship heading northeast toward the British Isles. After submerging and maneuvering into position, he fired four bow torpedoes at the zigzagging merchantman. Two detonations were heard by the sub's sound operator.

Surfacing, Greger observed the wounded steamer listing heavily to port. U-85 immediately submerged and moved closer to the damaged ship. Surfacing 20 minutes later, the bridge watch was unable to locate the vessel and assumed that it had sunk. U-85 searched for debris for about five hours without success. The target merchantman, later identified as the *Port Wyndham*, escaped and sailed into a British port 10 days later.

Traveling on the surface most of the time, the weather for January was almost perfect. U-85 continued along on a westerly course for three more days, sighting but not attacking two steamers. The boat was in mid-ocean and equidistant from Lorient on the Occupied French Coast and New York. She had been at sea 15 days.

Another steamer was sighted on the 22nd and U-85 pursued her on the surface for three hours. Unable to catch the fast motor ship, the U-boat returned to her old course and speed.

Finally on the 24th, a suspicious vessel was sighted dead in the water. The men waited at their battle stations ready to sink what looked like an easy target but the U-boat did not attack. Greger ordered the boat turned toward the northwest on a course for St. Johns, Newfounderland. He was well aware of British submarine traps disguised as helpless merchantmen and decided not to take a chance that could result in him being sunk.

By the 27th U-85 was less than 150 miles from the coast of Newfounderland. On the 28th the sub was attacked by an aircraft but not damaged.

Cruising southwest and parallel to the shoreline, U-85 had still not found a target.

The next vessel was sighted on February 1st, but escaped in a rainsquall. By the 3rd the boat was just 100 miles southeast of Boston and still had not fired a single torpedo. On the 5th she was forced to submerge twice after sighting aircraft.

Turning northeast and sailing back in the direction of St. Johns, U-85 finally spotted convoy ONS 61, 100 miles east of Cape Race on the 9th of February. The convoy was heading for New York. Ludwig Forster in U-654 joined Greger in pursuit of the inward bound convoy. Forster was able to sink the French escort *Alysse* but Greger was unable to catch the fast moving ships.

U-85 moved south for the next 10 hours, spotting a lone merchant ship just before dusk on the 9th. Before a successful attack could be made, the vessel fled and was pursued on the surface by U-85. After a 7 hour chase, the U-boat submerged and maneuvered into position to launch her bow torpedoes. At 2020 hours, Greger fired a spread of 3 fish at the 5408-ton *Empire Fusselier*. The ship sank immediately, hit by one of the 3 torpedoes fired from U-85s bow tubes. Pursuit of the convoy was continued until an airplane alarm forced the submarine to submerge.

The next day, the 10th of February, Greger turned the U-85 due east and started the 1000-mile trip home. He had sunk only one ship but was low on fuel. He brought the U-85 safely into St. Nazaire on February 23, 1942.

Fourth War Cruise

Leaving St. Nazaire on March 21, U-85 began its 4th and final war cruise bound for the east coast of the United States. On-board, Greger carried two recently updated versions of the three-wheel *enigma* machine, designated *Schlussel* M by the *Kriegsmarine*. These new four-wheel machines that had been in service since February would cause a virtual intelligence blackout for Bletchley Park and allow U-85 to proceed into the Atlantic undetected. To avoid being spotted by British search planes and destroyers operating in and over the Bay of Biscay, the boat traveled submerged during daylight hours for the first three days out. On the 4th day, Greger decided that it was safe to proceed on the surface. For the next week, the sea was as smooth as a tabletop and the crew enjoyed fine weather, often sunning themselves on the deck.

By the 29th, the wind had risen to gale force and heavy seas caused the torpedoes to shift inside the U-boat. The men also learned that their base at St. Nazaire had been attacked by British commandos and heavily damaged. On the 30th the constant rolling in the heavy swells damaged the electric motors.

Finally on the 31st the storm broke and tranquil weather returned. For the next week, the men were able to again enjoy the calm seas and warm weather.

On April 7th, Greger approached his assigned station near the coast of the United States east of

New York. He announced to the men that the boat was about 300 nautical miles from land and 660 nautical miles from Washington.

Cruising south on the surface the night of the 9th, a blinking buoy spotted by the lookouts caused an alarm to be sounded and the U-boats crew brought to battle stations. The following

Wild boar on the U-85's con.

night, the lookouts spotted more lights, but this time the lights were the navigation lights of a small freighter running south through the calm

seas. Greger fired two torpedoes, sinking her with two hits. She was the 5,000-ton Swedish freighter *Christina Knudsen* in route to New Orleans.

Still moving south for the next three days, the submarine lay on the bottom during daylight hours and surfacing at night to search for shipping. By the evening of April 13, U-85 was east of Hampton Roads and the Chesapeake Bay. Running on the surface and moving south over the calm seas, the U-boat reached a position about 15 miles northeast of Oregon Inlet, North Carolina near midnight. Unknown to Captain

Greger, the Navy destroyer U. S. S. *Roper* was only a few miles behind him on anti-submarine patrol and slowly closing on his position. Just after midnight the two warships would meet.

The officers of U-85 from left to right Oberleutnant zur see Helmut Lechler Oberleutnant zur see Hans Sanger Oberleutnant zur see Eberhard Greger Leutnant zur see Wolfgang Komorowski Courtesy Matthias Vogt

U. S. S. Roper (DD 147) commanded by Lt. Commander Hamilton Howe. Thanks to a newly installed radar unit on the ship that Greger was unaware of, Howe caught the U-85 on the surface and sank her. Courtesy Homer Hickam.

The Sinking of U-85

"The submarine war is in a way like big game hunting, but within seconds the hunter becomes the hunted and has to run for his life. Being hunted requires what I call second-stage thinking, calculating what your opponent thinks you will do and then doing the opposite. Sometimes it is like a game of chess, especially if your opponent has experience and knows the rules of the game. The stakes are high, of course."

Jurgen Oesten
Commander of U-61,
U-106 and U-861

U.S.S Roper

Captain Hamilton Howe, the commander of *U. S. S. Roper* (DD147), one of seven destroyers released from convoy duty for antisubmarine patrol, was quickly learning the rules of the game. His ship was nearby the night her companion destroyer *Jacob Jones* was sunk without warning by two German torpedoes from the U-578 in the early morning hours of February 28th, 1942.

Roper was a vintage "four-pipe" destroyer launched in August of 1918. She was 315 feet long and had a displacement of 1,600 tons. The ship had a 115-man crew and was armed with five 3-inch guns, four .50-caliber machine guns, and six torpedoes; 2 racks of depth charges, and Y and K-guns for propelling the charges over a wide area. She had a top speed of 28 knots, enabling her to outrun a U-boat traveling all out at 17 knots on the surface. She was also equipped with radar, a piece of equipment that the *Jacob Jones* did not have and of which the U-85 was unaware.

On the night of April 13, *Roper* steamed away from the naval base at Norfolk, Va. and headed out into the Atlantic on anti-submarine patrol. The ship was under the command of Lieutenant Commander Hamilton W. Howe, a 1926 graduate of the Naval Academy and close friend of Commander David Black. Black had been the Captain of the *Jacob Jones,* and was killed along with most of his men, when she was sunk by the U-578 in February. Commander Stanley C. Norton, commander of Destroyer Division 54 of which *Roper* was the flagship, was also onboard.

The night was clear and the wind calm as the zig-zagging *Roper* cleared Hampton Roads and motored southeast, parallel to the Virginia-North Carolina coastline. Around 11 o'clock, Commander Howe decided to turn in and let the officer of the deck, Kenneth Tebo take command of the vessel. Tebo continued along uneventfully on a southerly course for the next hour or so, and most of the *Roper's* crew not on watch, turned in for the night. The sky was beautiful and the calm sea full of phosphorescence. As midnight passed, the lookouts could see Bodie Island light and the #8 Bodie Island lighted buoy off to the southwest. The tranquil evening was about to change.

April 14, 1942

Roper's first radar contact with U-85 came at 6 minutes after midnight on April 14, 1942 when the U-boat was about 3000 yards away. The *Roper* was making 18 knots and on a course of 182 degrees true. Soon after the radar contact was made, Seaman Black, the destroyer's sonar operator began to hear U-85's high velocity propeller noise, and computed a range and bearing identical to those observed by the radar operator, Ensign Jim Mouquin. Howe was awakened and advised of the situation. He doubted that the contact was

Diary of Erich Degenkolb

A crewman aboard U-85 when it was sunk.

Calendar for year 1942.
Inscription: Fortune favors the efficient in the long run.

Jan. 1) Hilgegard Anhut   U-boat home Lorient   Organization Todt-
          good evening of dancing.
      2) Nothing special   a lot of work.
      3) Good orchestra   U-boat home.
      4) Same.
      5) Clean ship at sea.
      6) Letter from home.
     10) We sail.
     11) A/C alarm   getting warmer.   Seasick   Oh Neptune.
     12) Badly seasick.
     13) No end to it.
     14) Sanchan Sorensen's birthday 1925.
     15) Slowly getting better.
     16) Good weather.
     17) All up and well.
     18) First steamer sighted   got away.
     19) Horrible seas.
     20) Food tastes good again.
     21) Evening 7.35   a 10,000 ton ship sunk with a fan of four.
     22) Action stations early   Steamer escapes at full speed.
     23) 4/5 speed after it   couldn't catch it.
     24) Calm weather   11.00 in evening action stations.   My beard is
          growing noticeably.   The first German U-boats off the
          American coast.
     25) Quiet day.
     26) It is getting much cooler.
     27) Baptism of fire   A/C attack.
     28) Below Zero.
     29) Abominably cold   hardly bearable.
     30) Hitler speaks   off Newfounderland.
     31) Heavy seas   barometer rising and falling   we are off New York.

Feb. 1) 10,000 ton tanker sighted - ran away from us.
      2) Good weather - quiet day - 24.30 hurrah for home.
      3) Sea quite flat - took pictures.
     23) We reach home after successful cruise.

March 1) On leave.
     14) Back again.
     21) 18.00 we leave from St. Nazaire.
     22) We cruise submerged   in the distance depth charges.
     23) Submerged   quiet.
     24) We cruise on surface   magnificent weather.
     25) Sea as smooth as a table.
     26) Magnificent sunrise.
     27) The wind comes up   seasickness easy to find.
     28) Barometer rising   special announcement   landing at St. Nazaire.
     29) Torpedoes shift in heavy seas and beautiful music. Special
          announcement   116,000 tons sunk.
     30) Cut in electric motors   heavy seas   sighted whales.
     31) Quiet weather   nothing important.

April 1) Crashes. Inclination 55° St. B. or bearing 55° St. B.
      2) Changeable weather   rain.
      3) Light swell   magnificent sunshine.
      4) We aim torpedoes   cold   sea smooth big cake   baking.
          Abominable heat in the Gulf Stream.
      5) Noon   magnificent sunshine just off America. Thoughts of home.
      6) Night sky   still day light.
      7) 300 nautical miles from land.   660 to Washington.
      8) Abominable heat. All stripped bare.
      9) Alarm - before a buoy.   6 above zero.
     10) A steamer sighted and sunk 0100. fan of 2   2 hits.
     11) 1240   50 meters depth.   Off Washington - We cruise submerged.
          1830 - 8.5 meters under keel.   3 weeks at sea   3 steamers heard.
     12) We lie on bottom all day.   All is asleep off New York.
     13) American beacons and searchlights visible at night.

anything more than a fishing or Coast Guard patrol boat, but decided to let Tebo pursue it just for practice.

As the distance between the two vessels narrowed to less than 2100 yards, a small silhouette and wake were seen by the lookouts on the bridge of the *Roper*. The unknown vessel appeared to be running away at high speed. The wake suddenly turned sharply to port and then to starboard. At this point Tebo was convinced that the unidentified vessel was a U-boat and increased the destroyer's speed to 20 knots. He also knew that German submarines had stern torpedo tubes, and ordered the destroyer to move starboard of the contact's wake, and out of a direct line of fire. By this time Commander Howe and Commander Norton were on the bridge and following the action. Howe still did not order General Quarters. More time passed as the destroyer slowly closed on the still unidentified vessel.

When the range was reduced to about 700 yards, the track of a 3000-pound torpedo fired from U-85's stern torpedo tube passed close to the port side of the destroyer. Howe now ordered General Quarters, and the *Roper's* crew began readying themselves and the ship for a fight. Tebo, still in charge of the bridge, increased speed again, and continued the chase for another few minutes. As the range continued to decrease, *Roper's* 24-inch searchlight was switched on and U-85 was finally seen about 300 yards ahead, still turning to starboard.

Realizing that he had been found, Greger continued to turn U-85 to starboard inside the turning circle of the destroyer. He may have been trying to maneuver into position for a bow torpedo shot, but it was to late for that now. The water here was only 100 feet deep. Greger had to either scuttle and surrender, or fight it out on the surface. He chose to fight. The 88mm. gun crew poured out of the conning tower and headed for the deck gun.

On the destroyer, Chief Boatswains mate Jack Wright opened fire with his 50-caliber machine gun, raking the submarine with tracers and preventing the gun crew from reaching the 88mm. deck gun. The other three heavy machine guns on the *Roper* either jammed or misfired and could not be brought into action.

As the U-boat continued to turn, *Roper's* searchlight illuminated several crewmen jumping from the submarine into the Atlantic while others still desperately tried to man the deck gun. Wright continued fire-keeping most of the sub's crew pinned behind the conning tower.

Minutes later when the two vessels were side-to-side and only several hundred yards apart, U-85 slowed and stopped dead in the water. The *Roper* also slowed to keep the U-boat in sight as Harry Heyman and his gun crew readied their #5 three-inch gun. Heyman, the gun captain, yelled "fire" and an armor piercing shell was sent screaming toward the U-85. A moment later, an orange flash was seen on the aft end of the sub's conning tower by the men on the *Roper*. While Heyman and Wright continued to fire, a steady stream of Germans squeezed out of their conning tower hatch and jumped into the sea.

Executive Officer Vancus observed at least 35 crewmen in the water as U-85 rapidly sank stern first. Commander Howe later noted in his report that "about 40 of the U-boat's crew were sighted in the sea". Whether the direct hit by Harry Heyman's No. 5 gun, or an order from Greger to scuttle and abandon ship caused U-85 to sink is still unknown.

Although the blast from the three-inch shell penetrated the pressure hull above the control room and caused flooding, the penetration was small and probably could not have caused the submarine to sink as fast as it did. Sensing that U-85 was finished, Captain Greger most likely ordered the boat scuttled as the crew scrambled to exit the sinking U-boat. What happened to him is still a mystery.

As U-85's deck disappeared beneath the sea surface, most of the crew had already jumped into the near freezing ocean. The *Roper,* now less than 100 yards from the spot where U-85 sank, powered ahead through a sea of German sailors, all wearing life vests and calling for help. A life raft was ordered dropped from the *Roper,* but it became fouled in the rigging. Before the destroyer could circle again, a sonar contact caused the decision to be made by Commander Howe not to stop and attempt a rescue. Another U-boat could be nearby ready to sink the stopped destroyer. The *Jacob Jones* disaster was still fresh in Howe's memory and he had his own ship and men to think about. Instead of dropping a life raft, a pattern of 11 depth charges was sent flying from the Y and K guns toward the spot where U-85 went down. The 500-pound charges were set to explode at 50 feet and killed all of the survivors floating in the water.

The destroyer circled again and then slowed and turned off the searchlight. For the rest of the night, *Roper* remained in the area, searching and listening. Commander Norton retired to his cabin and wrote his report. The men of the *Roper* had made the first American U-boat kill of World War II by an American warship.

The following morning, two planes and a blimp arrived from the Coast Guard base near Elizabeth City and dropped smoke floats near a large oil slick rising from the U-85. Many bodies and debris were spotted floating in the water. At one time, at least seven planes and a blimp circled the area. The *Roper* dropped six more depth charges over the oil slick before stopping near the floats to pick up the bodies and other debris from the sunken U-boat. Twenty-nine dead sailors were recovered but Captain Greger was not among them. Two bodies were so badly damaged that they were allowed to sink after being searched. Diaries kept by seamen Eric Degenkolb and Eugen Ungethum were also found in the sea, revealing much about life on the U-85 and it's four war cruises.

After dropping a large orange buoy near the spot where U-85 went down, the *Roper* returned to Norfolk, and the bodies and diaries were turned over to Naval Intelligence. Several days later, the 29 dead German sailors were buried at Hampton National Cemetery near Newport News, Virginia.

What happened to the 15 U-boat crewmen not accounted for? No human remains have ever been found on the U-85. Stories of German U-boat men reaching the coast in rubber rafts soon after the sinking have never been disproved. Did some of U-85's crew escape and reach the mainland? Probably not. Commander Howe observed "about 40 men" in the water as the U-boat went down. The rest were most likely killed by machine gun fire and fell into the sea.

U-85 crewmen are buried
at Hampton National Cementery.

Lieutenant Commander Hamilton Howe receives the
Navy Cross from Admiral Andrews. Courtesy Bill Hughes.

Commander Howe and Commander Norton prepare their reports on board
The *Roper* following the sinking of U-85. Courtesy National Archives.

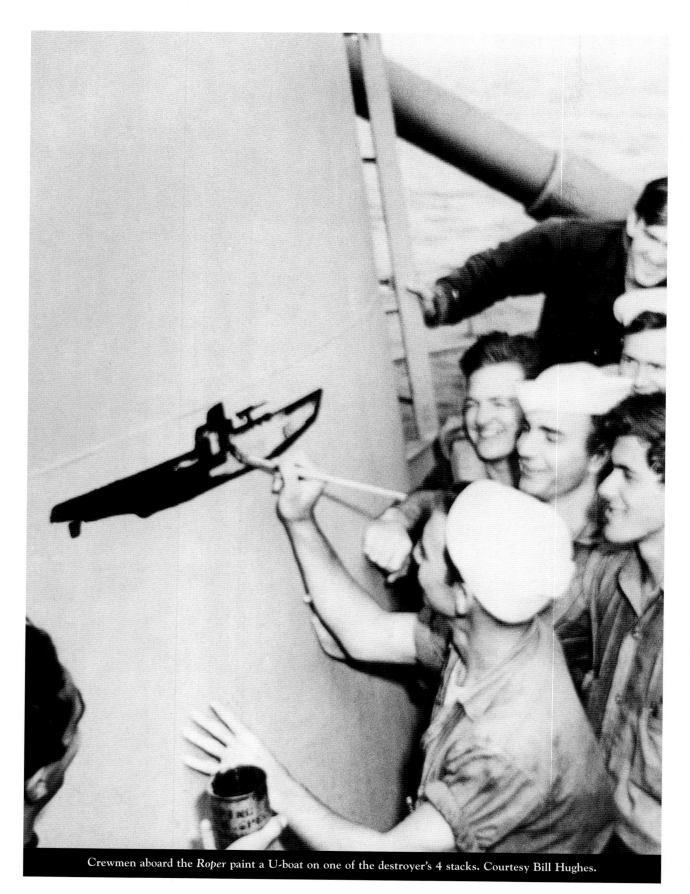

Crewmen aboard the *Roper* paint a U-boat on one of the destroyer's 4 stacks. Courtesy Bill Hughes.

Rhodes Chamberlin

It's April 13, 1942 - the start of another week or so of antisubmarine patrol off Cape Hatteras. That evening I had the 8-12 watch in the Radio shack and being inside copying our "Fox" skeds I didn't know that *Roper* had picked up a radar contact of some small vessel ahead of us and that we were investigating, nor did I know until after GQ sounded that our radar contact was a submarine which had launched at least one torpedo at us from its stern tubes. So after being relieved, I had just gotten below in the after living compartment when GQ sounded. Being just at the base of the after compartment ladder, I was the first man topside and out of the After Deck House on the starboard side just aft of Number 5 gun. The 24-inch searchlight was illuminating a submarine about 300 yards off our starboard side. Number 5's 3 inch gun was just starting to be manned as a half dozen or so men on the sub showed up on their deck heading for their guns, a 20mm on the conning tower and a 88mm forward. Almost immediately one of our 50 cal. Machine guns on the Galley Deck House started firing, going back and forth as the sub sailors ran in and out from

Rhodes Chamberlin 1942. Courtesy Rhodes Chamberlin.

behind their conning tower as they tried to man their guns. Our Number 3 3 inch on the Galley Deck House had misfired 3 times with a projectile jammed in the barrel on its last try. Meanwhile Chief Boatswains Mate Jack E. Wright who was manning the 50 cal. Machine fun, which was right next to No. 3 gun, continued aking back and forth on the sub deck with the sub sailors still trying to man their guns. By this time No. 5 was manned and Gun Captain Harry Heyman had his gun trained out and had started to fire. The third shell struck the sub at the base of the aft end of the conning tower. There was an explosion with a large spray of water, a sight I can still see plainly in my minds eye. Moments later the sub started to sink, going down aft first. There were still only about 10 or 12 sailors topside.

After watching a few more moments I went forward, arriving on the Well Deck, just as we approached, having continued our circling, a group of survivors. I could see some of them just a few feet away. Someone called down from the bridge to release the large life raft, which was on a set of ways just overhead. I pulled the lanyard to release the raft when the small stuff which holds the center platform to the outer ring caught on the ways. I was in the process of cutting it loose when the bridge called down again to hold till next time around. Unfortunately a sound contact caused the decision to drop a pattern of depth charged which killed all of the survivors in the water. The next morning we picked up 29 bodies. Later that day they were all transferred to the *USS Scioto*, which took them into NOB Norfolk.

I have often thought of the U-85 sinking and especially of the sight of our shell hitting the submarine. I have collected a number of accounts of it, all written be men who weren't there and all had some parts that were inaccurate. It took being contacted by Richard Reichenbacher who had dove on U-85 a number of times and was interested in my recollections of the sinking that really stirred my memories and gave me a very strong desire to revisit the scene.

So I got myself certified as an Open Water Diver and with Richard and Marty Bailey (who was to be my dive buddy) traveled to Nags Head. With the help of Sea Scan Dive Center and Rich and Roger Hunting who gave us a boat ride, I was back where it all happened. Going down the line towards the U-85 and then having her come into view lying there on the bottom was a real thrill. Reaching the U-85's remains I was at last able to see and put my arm into the hole which 58 years before I had seen blown into U-85's hull that I still remember so vividly.

Rhodes Chamberlin
14 Feb. 2001
El Paso, Texas

Bert Miller, 1942. Courtesy Bert Miller.

Bert Miller, 1984 visiting the gravesites of U-85 crewmen at
Hampton National Cementary.

The *Falcon* rescuing crewmen from the U. S. Submarine *Squalus*. Courtesy Bert Miller.

The First Divers

Within 24 hours after U-85 went down, divers and equipment from the experimental diving unit in Washington D. C. had been flown to the Naval Operation Base at Norfolk, Va., and were on board the British trawler *H. M. S. Bedfordshire* steaming toward the spot where the submarine was sunk. Since U-85 was lying in about 100 feet of water, the Navy hoped that the U-boat could be refloated and salvaged.

H. M. S. Bedfordshire

Arriving at position 35 degrees 55 N, 75 degrees 19 W. and the orange marker buoy left by the *Roper*, the first diver was lowered from the *Bedfordshire* on April 16, 1942. The following day, diver number six found the U-85. Visibility was poor and the diver could not identify what part of the boat he was on. Due to increasingly bad weather, no more attempts were made to reach the submarine during the next five days.

The *Bedfordshire*, on loan to the United States from Great Britain and soon to be sunk near Ocracoke, N. C. by the U-558, returned to convoy escort duty on April 20th and was replaced by the *U. S. S. Kewaydin*. Resuming diving operations from this ship on April 22nd, the second diver down found an unexploded American Mark V1 depth charge lying next to the starboard side of the U-boat, again halting all diving until this charge was destroyed four days later by the Navy's mine disposal unit.

U. S. S. Falcon

Seven more dives were made from the *Kewaydin* and several buoyed lines were finally attached to the wreck before the diving and salvage vessel *U. S. S. Falcon* arrived at daybreak Wednesday, April 29th, 1942.

With Navy and Coast Guard escort vessels circling, WWI submarine veteran Bert Miller made the first dive to the U-85 from the *Falcon* at noon on April 30, 1942. Miller, using a Mark V deep sea rig, dropped through the 100 feet of water to the submarine in about two minutes.

"When I reached the 85, the sun was shining bright on it, and the first thing I saw was a wild boar's head with a rose in its mouth, painted on the conning tower. The way the sun hit it, it was a beautiful sight underwater that I'll never forget. I wish I'd had a camera," Miller said. What Miller saw was the insignia painted on the U-boat by Lothar-Guenther Buchheim the previous summer.

Miller, whose dive lasted about one hour, made a visual inspection of the U-boat and found no major damage. He entered the conning tower and found the control room hatch closed but not dogged. Opening this hatch, he looked into the control room and claimed that he was greeted by American occupation money floating in the flooded compartment.

During the next five days, 78 dives were made to the U-85 from the *Falcon*. Gauges, instruments, the 20mm. anti-aircraft gun on the bridge, and the gun sights from the 88mm. deck-gun were removed. An attempt was also made to remove the aft torpedo storage container and torpedo, but was unsuccessful. Several attempts to blow air into the diving and ballast tanks were also unsuccessful due to collapsed piping from depth charging.

On May 4th, 1942, Ltd. G. K. Mackenzie Jr., commanding officer aboard the *Falcon*, ended the diving operation after gathering the following information about the sunken submarine: The U-85 was listing about 80 degrees to starboard, all internal compartments were flooded with flood valves and vents open, except number two port and starboard, which was apparently secured as a reserve fuel tank; the forward torpedo tubes were loaded, with muzzle doors open; the hull and superstructure were undamaged except for holing by shell fire on the starboard side; the bow and stern planes were undamaged; the U-85 was scuttled by her crew, and successful salvage could only be accomplished by extensive pontooning.

After recovering tools, mooring lines, and anchors, the *Falcon* and her escorts returned to the Naval Operations Base in Norfolk Va., leaving only a large red buoy marked "A", attached to a quarter inch line from U85's conning tower.

USS *Falcon,* a diving and salvage vessel built in the early 1900's, arrived on the scene of U-85's sinking on April 29th, 1942. More than 80 dives were made from this ship to the U-85 before leaving the site on May 4.

A diver holds on to ready the ammunition container being hauled to the surface from U-85's deck.
Courtesy Michael A. deCamp

Revisited In The 60s

When the Navy left the U-85 in 1942, latitude and longitude coordinates of the submarine were documented in the *Falcons* official report. Although this was the best method of positioning at the time, it was not exact enough to re-locate the wreck without a lot of guesswork and extensive searching with a fathometer.

Ray Wingate

In the late 1960s Ray Wingate, a Virginia Beach commercial fisherman, became interested in the U-85 for its fishing potential. Researching the Navy records documenting the sinking, he was able to convert latitude and longitude coordinates of the submarine to coordinates used in a new method of positioning called Loran-A. With these coordinates and a fathometer, Wingate found what he believed was the U-85.

Although Wingate was not a diver, his friend, Rod Wagner was. Wagner a retired UDT adventurer enjoyed exploring new wrecks found by Wingate. Rod would search the wrecks for fish and direct Ray to the best spots for fishing.

Shortly after Wingate's discovery of what he thought was the U-85, he and Wagner returned to the site. Wagner dove and confirmed that the wreck was the German submarine. A brass flare gun with U-85 inscribed in the metal was proof enough.

For the next several years, Wagner dove and Wingate fished the U-85.

Art LePage

Around 1975, Art LePage, a Wanchese salvage diver, learned of Wingate's trips to the wreck and chartered his boat for a week of diving the U-85. LePage, owner then of the Outer Banks Dive Shop, was impressed with the wreck's sport diving poten-

Jim Bunch and Captain Art Lepage

tial, and immediately hired Wingate to begin scheduled charter service to the submarine.

Larry Keen

Captain Larry Keen, a native of Ocean City Maryland, also began organizing charters to the U-85 in the mid 1970s. He and his dive boat *Gekos* have undoubtedly taken more divers to the U-85 over the past 30 years than all other operators combined. He still spends several weeks each summer taking divers to the U-85.

The *Sea Fox* anchored above the U-85.

Captain Larry Keen heading for the U-85.

During the years that have followed, charters to the wreck have usually been available May through September. The number of divers visiting the U-85 has steadily increased from only a handful before 1980, to several hundred a season now. It is one of only three U-boats that are regularly visited off the Atlantic Coast of the United States.

(The above account of the U-85 discovery was provided by Captain Art LePage)

Sea Fox

Jim Stuart brought the 50 foot dive boat *Sea Fox* from the Florida Keys to Dare County in the spring of 1977. The boat operated here seasonally over the next 25 years taking hundreds of divers to the U-85 and other local shipwrecks. Captained first by Stuart and followed by Captains Dougie Pledger, Tom Hardy, and Mike Andrews, the *Sea Fox* returned to Florida in 2001.

The *Gekos* circles above the U-85.

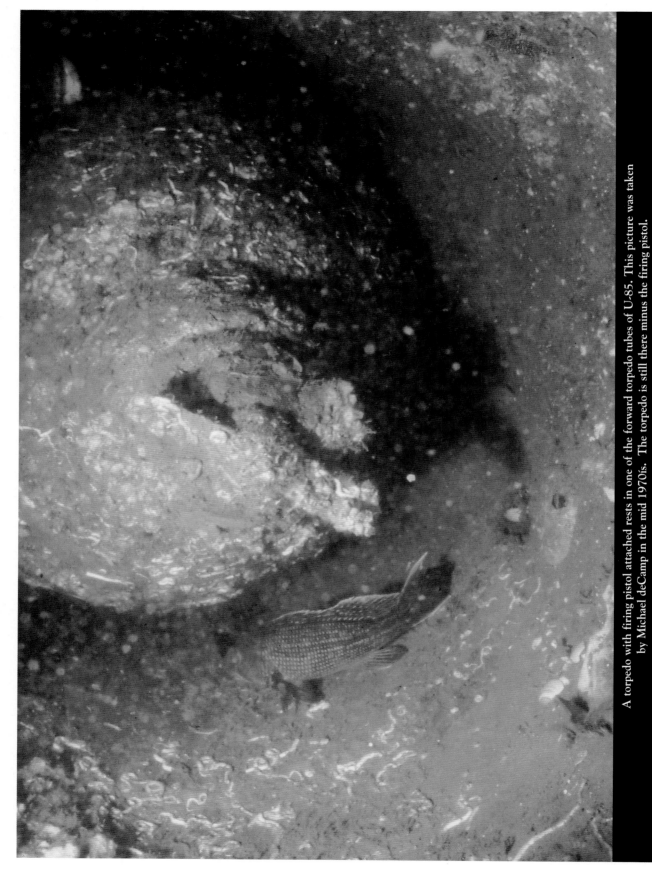

A torpedo with firing pistol attached rests in one of the forward torpedo tubes of U-85. This picture was taken by Michael deCamp in the mid 1970's. The torpedo is still there minus the firing pistol.

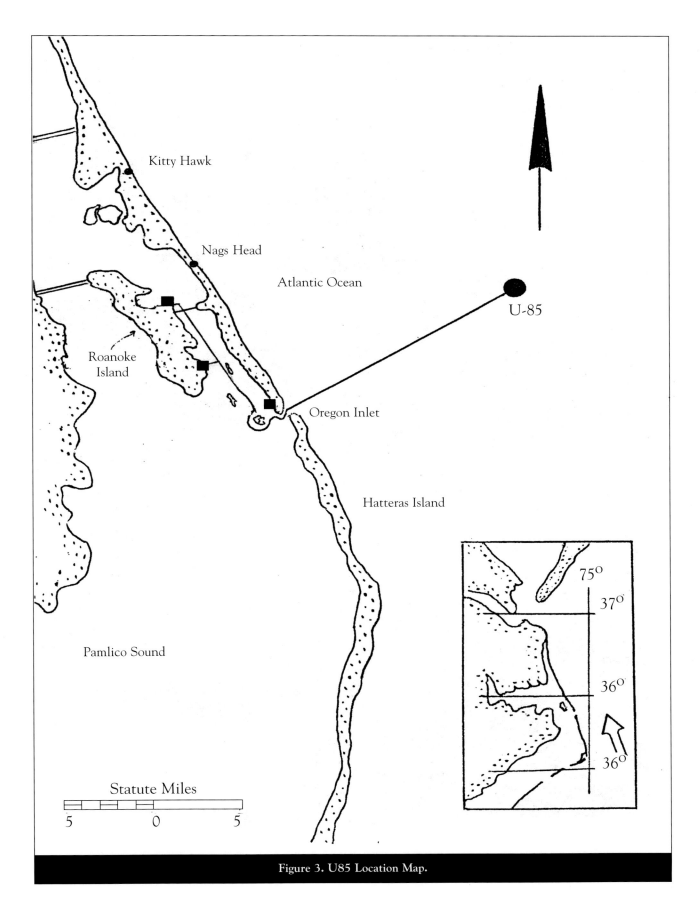

Figure 3. U85 Location Map.

Divers approaching the U-85. Glenn Eure

Roger Hunting, Jim Bunch, and Rich Hunting ready to dive the U-85.

Diving the U-85

Getting There

U-85 is a small shipwreck, a tiny object on the bottom of a big ocean. There is no permanent anchorage marking it's location. Finding the wreck and anchoring here is difficult if not impossible for all but the most experienced boaters. It is no easy task.

Boats traveling to the U-85 leave from The Oregon Inlet Fishing Center, Thicket Lump Marina, Wanchese Harbor, Pirates Cove Marina, and several other docking areas on the Roanoke Sound. As much as a 50 mile round trip and 3 hour boat ride can be expected if leaving from the more distant points of Manteo or Pirates Cove.

Locating U-85

U-85 lies on the sandy bottom a little more than 12 miles east-northeast of the sea buoy marking the entrance to Oregon Inlet. A course of 65 degrees from this buoy will get you there. Until recently, the Loran-C coordinates 17.0, 13.5 were used to pinpoint the exact location of the wreck. The G. P. S. or Ground Positioning System, a more accurate and reliable navigational tool, is used by most boaters today.

Both fishing and dive boats visit the U-85. For years, offshore charter Captains have left the dock at three A. M., determined to reach the fishing grounds ahead of the other boats. Dive boats do the same thing. Its not unusual for several boats heading for the same wreck to engage in friendly competition trying to reach the wreck site first.

Being the first to reach the U-85 is especially important because the wreck is so small. Nothing is more disheartening than spotting a tiny spec on the sea over the spot where the U-85 is located. Moving closer, the spec takes on the shape of a lone boat sitting at anchor above the wreck, confirming the fear that someone else has beaten you to the U-85.

Occasionally I have watched several boats converging a few miles from the wreck. This is when the captains realize that all are heading for the same place, the U-85. The race is on. On a calm day, the fastest boat wins. On a rough day, the largest boat wins. On many days, all boats arrive at about the same time.

Hooking The Wreck

Once the surface position above the wreck is reached, the real work begins. U-85's pressure hull, all that remains of the submarine, is only 160 feet long and 20 feet wide. Except for hatchways and the deck gun, the hull is for the most part a featureless cylinder very difficult to hook.

U-85's bow points toward the southeast with a 35 degree list to starboard. Sand has covered the port side bringing the ocean floor to the top of the pressure hull. This side is referred to as the "high side" and is very difficult to hook.

The bottom on the starboard side is a good 15 feet deeper and levels out at about 100 feet. The pressure hull on this side is more exposed and presents a better target for a dive boat's anchor. This side is called the "low side."

The first boat to "see" the wreck on it's fathometer drops an anchor. The mate clutches the line delicately as if waiting for a fish to bite. He is hoping to feel the bump-bump-bump of the chain and anchor bouncing over the steel pressure hull.

To successfully attach a line to the wreck, the

boat must maneuver in such a way that when the anchor is dropped, it will pass through the 100 feet of water, slide along the wreck, and hang on some part of the pressure hull. Wind direction, current velocity, wind speed, and sea state all play a part in how long it takes to complete this process.

Soon, if the hook doesn't catch, the anchor falls to the sand and is pulled away from the 85 by the drifting dive boat. The next boat in line, seeing that the wreck has not been hooked, maneuvers into position to drop anchor. This goes on until the wreck is hooked.

The other boats are out of luck unless they are invited by the Captain of the anchored boat to tie up behind him. This works O. K., but presents the added challenge of swimming on the surface to the anchored boat and then using the boat's descent line to reach the sub.

Hooking the wreck on the first try is like stepping up to the plate and hitting a home run. It happens only occasionally. Most of the time, 2 or 3 drops are necessary to "hook up." Retrieving 200 feet of rope and an anchor with 15 feet of chain is the penalty paid for each miss.

Each repositioning for the next try takes 5 to 15 minutes. This author has on more than one occasion, circled the U-85 for more than an hour trying to plant the hook.

On one memorable occasion in the mid-1980s a diver on the dive boat Sea Fox became irate when Captain Doogie Pledger was unable to hook the wreck because of huge seas and a cross current. Captain Pledger suggested moving to the Byron Benson, a larger and more accessible wreck. The diver exploded "I didn't pay to dive on a junk freighter." Captain Pledger finally succeeded in hooking the sub and completed the scheduled dives.

Fortunately for those interested in diving this wreck, the site is almost always free of other boats. Most of my dives on the wreck over the past 25 years were made when the only boat on the site was the one I was on.

Larry Keen and Jim Bunch on Keen's boat *Gekos*

Rich Hunting, Hugh Raulston, Billy Daniels, Roger Hunting

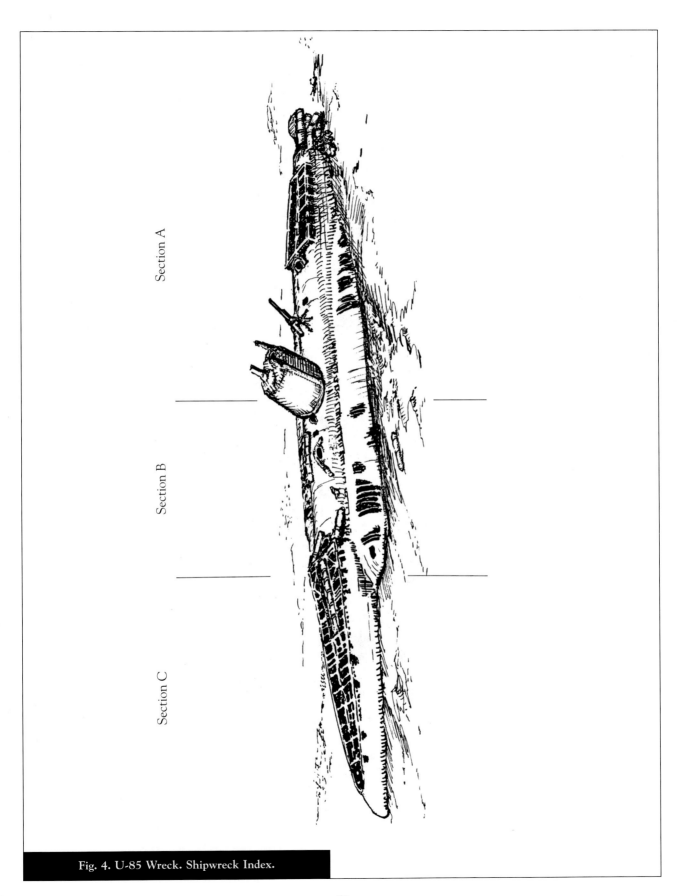

Section A

Section B

Section C

Fig. 4. U-85 Wreck. Shipwreck Index.

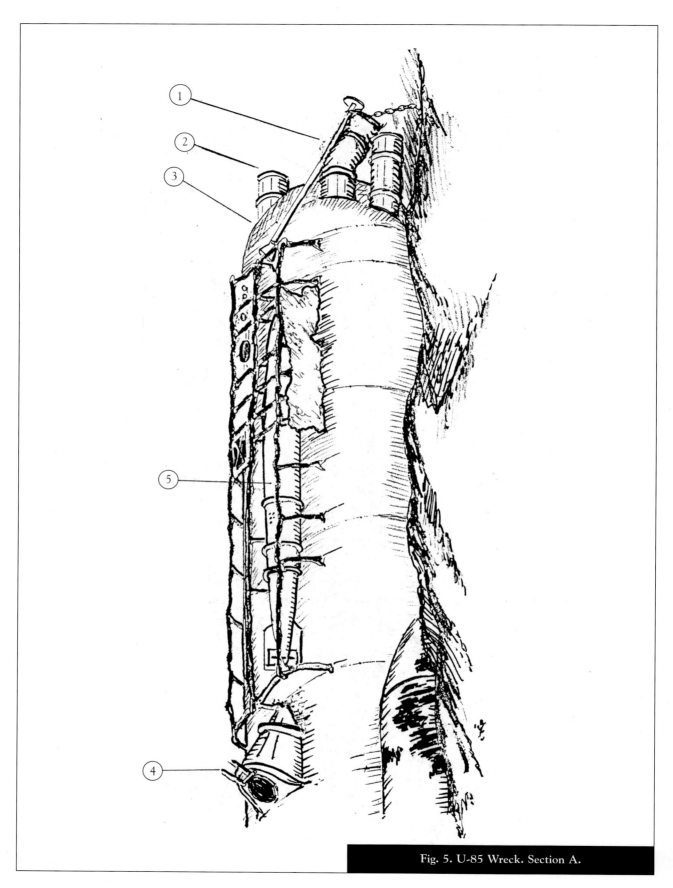

Fig. 5. U-85 Wreck. Section A.

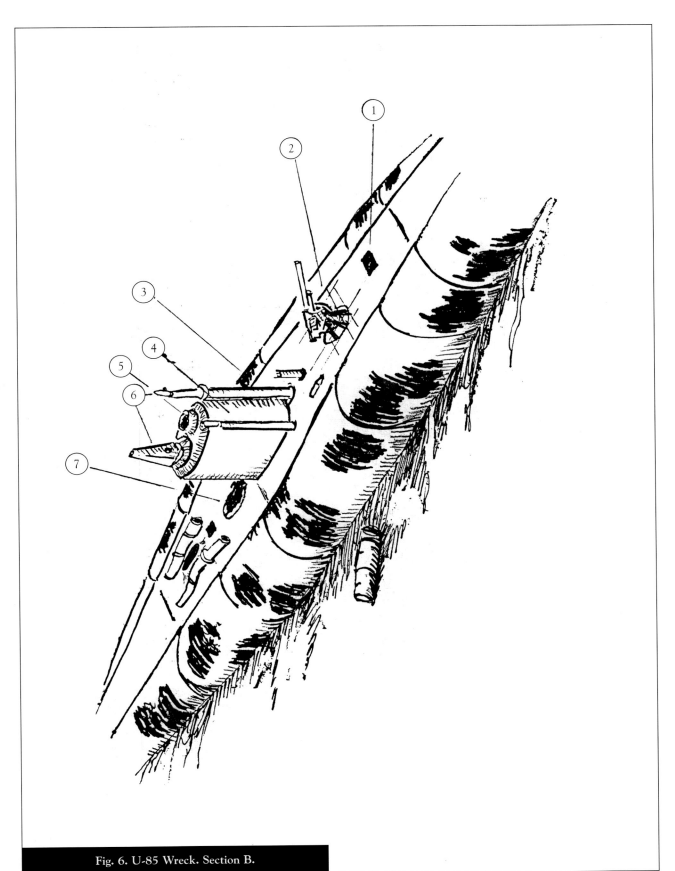

Fig. 6. U-85 Wreck. Section B.

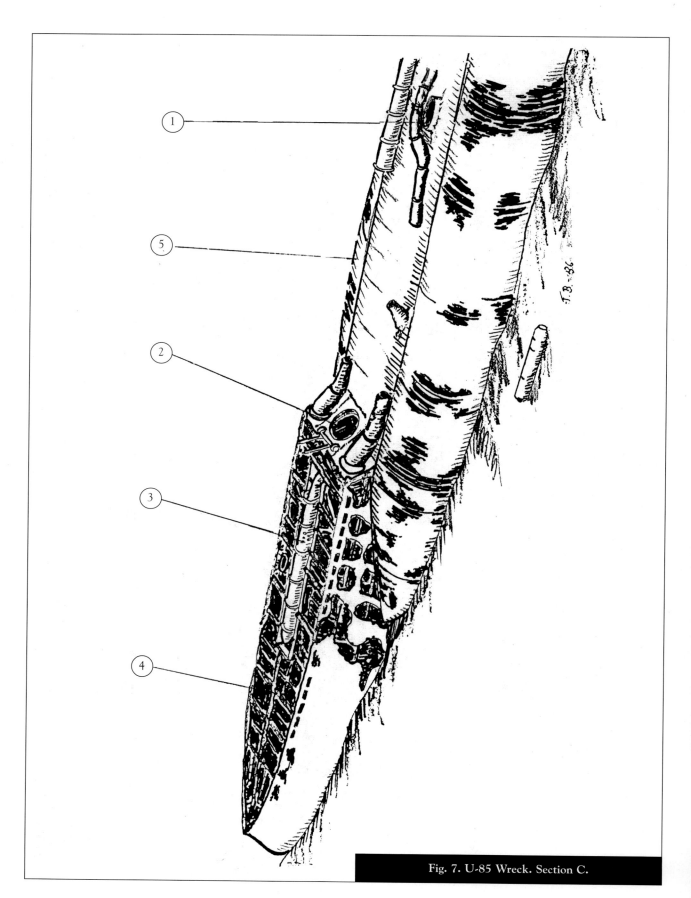

Fig. 7. U-85 Wreck. Section C.

Outside The U-85

A diver planning to explore the U-85 during the summer months can normally expect 65-degree bottom water, visibility of 20 to 50-feet, light or no bottom current, and depending on the air mix, a 20 or 30 minute dive at 100 feet.

Since the wreck's pressure hull is a little over 160-feet long and located in relatively deep water, one complete swim around will consume the majority of available bottom time.

Major Features Of Interest

Under average conditions, the major features of interest on the outside of U-85 can be seen during a single dive. These include: the forward four torpedo tubes with torpedoes inside, the forward diving planes, the 88mm. deck cannon, the conning tower and periscope masts, the hole through the pressure hull created by *Roper's* 3-inch shell, the G7a torpedo in the stern deck storage canister, and the seven open hatches leading inside the pressure hull.

A dive with the above objectives is typified in the following mid-summer visit to the U-85. The photos accompanying the description are keyed to figures 5, 6, and 7.

Once in the water, the swim down the descent line takes about two minutes. During the summer and early fall, huge schools of amberjack circle divers for the first 50 feet or so on the way down. These fish are large and come close enough to touch. Occasionally a porpoise will swim over the wreck and give divers a brief look before disappearing into the blue haze. The warm waters of late summer and early fall also attract curious barracuda that

will approach divers as they descend. Large numbers of sand tiger sharks visit the wreck in late spring but move on before the summer diving season.

The warm surface water and Caribbean-like visibility change when the thermocline is reached. Visibility usually drops to less than 30 feet and water temperature to less than 70 degrees. The water color gradually changes from deep blue to dark green as the shadow of U-85 comes into view. If conditions are good, the conning tower, deck gun, and bow with four torpedo tubes protruding through the pressure hull can be recognized from a vantage point 25 feet above the wreck. The absence of the thin outer faring and wooden decking that once covered the pressure hull and the two eroding saddle tanks straddling the pressure hull give the sub an unfinished appearance as the divers reach the submarine.

Approaching the bow, a look into the four torpedo tubes reveals the remains of the torpedoes that are still there. Shining a light inside here usually attracts the attention of several large conger eels living in the tubes (1, 2A). Salvagers blew off the bow casing that covered these tubes in an attempt to enter the forward torpedo room. Several high-pressure air cylinders, anchor chain, parts of the windlass mechanism and other debris rust away on the sandy bottom.

On the port side, just behind the torpedo tubes, the forward diving plane is angled downward in the dive position indicating that the boat was set for submerged running at the time she sank (3A).

Swimming along the mid-line of the pressure hull toward the stern, the first open hatch comes into view. This hatch, minus it's hatch-cover and angled at 45 degrees from the deck, is the forward torpedo-loading hatch (4A). This hatchway was used to load torpedoes into the forward torpedo room.

The reserve torpedo container that was just forward of this hatch and the G7a single bladed torpedo that was stored in it are gone (5A). The torpedo, which was here until the late 1980s mysteriously disappeared leaving a trail in the sand beside the submarine.

The next open hatch is several feet aft of the torpedo hatch and is rectangular in shape. This is the forward battery hatch and was used to load batteries that were stored below the flooring (1B). This hatch is directly above the officers quarters.

The most prominent feature attached to the pressure hull is the 88mm. deck gun (2B). This gun is right above and behind the battery hatch and has literally been taken to pieces by divers over the last 30 years. The many 88mm. rounds that littered the deck in the early 70s have long since disappeared.

Right behind the deck gun, a small 6-inch hole through the pressure hull leads into the control room, and once was fitted with a hollow mast connected to the deck mounted main magnetic compass. A mirror image of the compass rose was transmitted by light through the mast and projected on the face of a small screen in the control room. The gauge box that held the screen was just above the main steering station here.

The conning tower, located in the center of the pressure hull, extends 8 feet above the deck (4B). The bridge faring is gone, exposing the 1.2-inch thick steel around the attack center. The wintergarten was destroyed by a direct hit from the Roper. The 20mm. anti-aircraft gun that once stood on the wintergarten is also gone, recovered by Navy divers from the U.S.S. Falcon in 1942. The tower has started to separate from the hull and will probably fall to the sand before long.

The bridge access escape hatch cover and the access hatch cover between the attack center and the control room are gone. Looking through these hatches, the interior of the control room can be seen 16 feet below (5B).

The control room sky periscope mast, and the attack periscope well are attached to the conning tower pressure hull (6B). The sky periscope mast is forward and the attack well aft. The sky periscope head was removed in the seventies, but the attack periscope is still visible and retracted in the well.

Just behind the attack center where the Wintergarten was located, a large jagged hole in the pressure hull exposes the interior of the aft end of the control room (7B). The 3-inch shell from the Roper's deck gun scored the fatal hit here on U-85. The size of the opening gets larger each year.
Looking down from the top of the conning tower, the immense size of the saddle tanks straddling the pressure hull can be seen (8B). These tanks held both fuel and water for ballast and have almost completely rusted away.

The next recognizable feature behind the conning tower is the after battery hatch. This hatch is rectangular and about 10 feet from the conning tower. The hatch is very small but large enough to accommodate the batteries that were stored below the flooring here. Shining a light through this opening illuminates the remains of the senior rate's quarters.

Several feet behind this hatch and round in shape is the galley hatch (1C). This hatch is right above the small galley area. A small stove and the doorway into the engine room can be seen through this opening.
Moving aft past the galley hatch, the stern torpedo hatch makes a 45-degree angle with the pressure hull. (2C). This hatchway, that once served as an entrance for torpedoes that would be fired from

the single aft tube, is open but blocked by two large steel horizontal shafts on the inside of the pressure hull. Looking inside here, a diver can see the tops of the electric motors that powered the submarine while it was submerged.

Just behind this hatchway and along the centerline of the pressure hull, look for the remains of the stern torpedo storage container and a G7a torpedo (3C).

Approaching the stern, rudder control shafts can be seen through the deck casing (4C). The propellers, rudders, and hydroplanes are not visible, but are there, buried in the sand.

Pausing a minute before starting the 160-foot swim back to the bow, a quick compass check aligns the plane of U-85 in a southeast, northwest direction, with the bow southeast.

Heading northwest and over the port saddle tank, the bottom comes up almost to the top of the pressure hull, filling the broken tank compartments with sand (5C). The submarine has acted like a submerged breakwater, eroding the bottom on the starboard side and trapping it on the port side.

The swim back to the bow is a good time to enjoy the many species of fish and invertebrates that inhabit the nooks and crannies created here over the past 50 years.

Finally, passing over the port bow plane, the descent line comes into view. During the swim up the line, the same schools of amberjack that greeted the divers on the way down rejoin them on their way back to the surface. Passing through the thermocline, the cold dark green water changes to warm deep blue as the bottom of the dive boat appears above.

A diver hovers above the forward torpedo tubes. (1A)

Triggerfish swim between the starboard bow torpedo tubes. (1A

One of U-85's many conger eels in a forward torpedo tube. Courtesy Roger Hunting. (2A)

Forward port diving plane. Note the downward position indicating the U-85 was in a dive mode when sunk. (3A)

Kevin Bradshaw shines his light through the forward torpedo-loading hatch. (4A)

A G7a single bladed torpedo in the forward deck storage compartment. The torpedo was removed by the Navy in the mid 1980s. (5A)

Diver John Finelli emerges from the forward battery hatch (1B) Photo by Bill Hughes

88mm deck gun in the late 1970's. (2B)

John A. Watkins approaches the conning tower from the bow. (6B)

The conning tower hatch. (5B)

The conning tower extends 8 feet above the deck. (4B)

Large jagged hole in the pressure hull created by
a shell from *Roper's* 3-inch deck gun. (7B)

John A. Watkins shines his light into the
opening just above the control room. (7B)

Deterioration of the port saddle tank. (8B)

A diver looks into the galley hatch. (1C)

Stern torpedo loading hatch. (2C)

Stern torpedo storage container with torpedo inside. (3C)

Divers swim near the stern of U-85. (4C)

Lucy Fuller above broken port saddle tank. (5C)

Type VIIB Internal Profile and Plan

1. Forward torpedo tubes
2. Forward torpedo room
3. Forward torpedo hatch
4. Forward head
5. Food storage
6. Chief Petty Officers room
7. Wardroom and officers room
8. Captains room
9. Sound room
10. Radio room
11. Battery room
12. S-Great room
13. Magazine
14. Forward battery hatch
15. Control room
16. Conning tower
17. Sky periscope
18. Attack periscope
19. Conning tower hatch
20. Petty officers room
21. Aft battery hatch
22. Aft battery room
23. Galley hatch
24. Galley
25. Diesel engine room
26. Electric motor room
27. Aft torpedo hatch
28. Stern torpedo tube
29. Watertight ammunition container

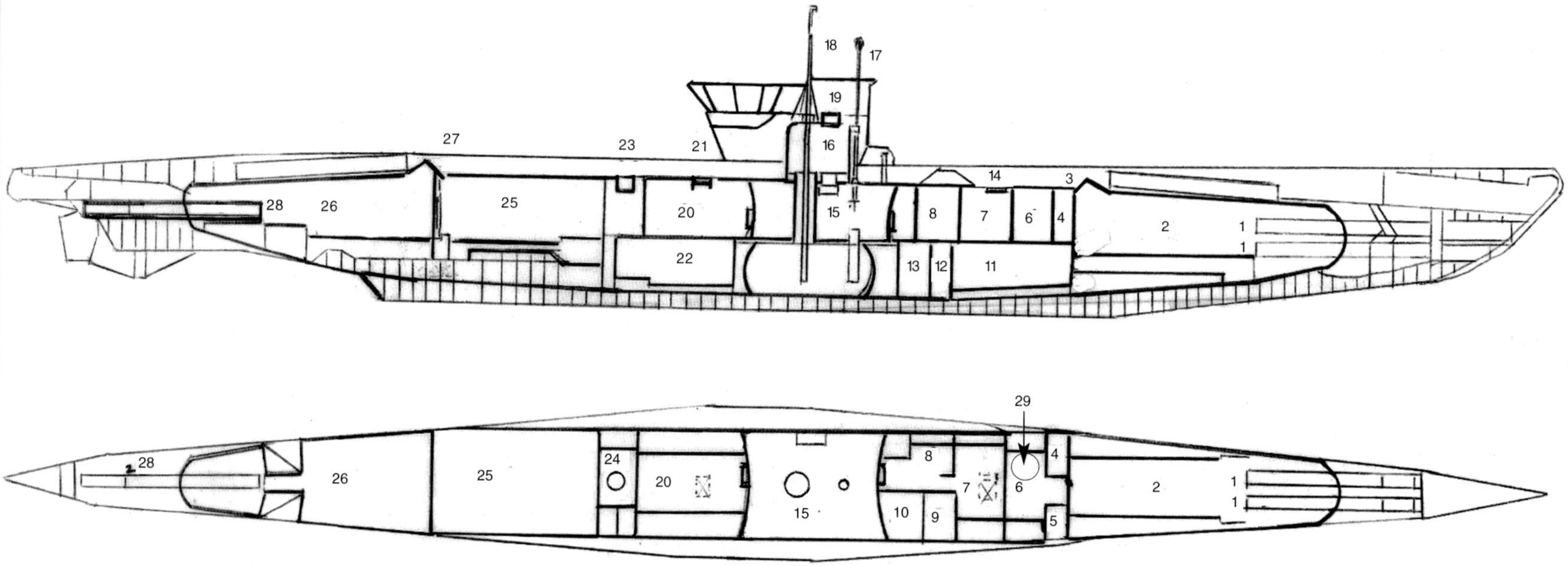

Figure 8. U-85 Internal Plan.

72

Inside The U-85

The following account of what remains inside the pressure hull of U-85 is not a guide for penetration dives on this wreck. The author does not recommend or advocate entry into this submarine. The information is provided only as a history of this diver's experience inside the U-85.

U-85's pressure hull has a list of about 35 degrees to starboard. This list is easy to see while swimming along the outside of the submarine and helps with orientation during periods of low visibility. On the inside, this is not the case. Since sand lies flat on U-85's floor, the perception that the hull is also positioned flat on the bottom seems logical. In reality, swimming from bow to stern, the center of the overhead is not straight up but tilted about 35 degrees to port. This increases the likelihood that a diver inside will become disoriented. It's very hard to visualize what should be where.

This list plus extreme deterioration of the sub's internal components and silting problems inside make it very difficult to recognize features that are easily identified in a picture or diagram. Only by making many visits to the same area can a diver finally recognize what he is actually looking at inside the U-85.

There are seven open hatches that allow entry into U-85's pressure hull. They are: the forward torpedo hatch, forward battery hatch, conning tower hatch, control room hatch, stern battery hatch, galley hatch, and the stern torpedo hatch. All of the hatch covers have been removed. The battery hatches are rectangular, the others round. All present a tight squeeze.

No matter which hatch a diver chooses to enter, it is impossible to swim the entire length of the pressure hull without exiting. This is because of the collapsed aft end of the control room and the large amount of sediment in the diesel and electric motor rooms.

It is always dark and cold inside. Endless entanglements and large conger eels, several over six-feet long, wait to intimidate anyone who enters. Digging or finning through the thick sediment on the floor always brings visibility to zero. Even the most careful movement by a diver inside can bring on a complete blackout and create an extreme exit problem. The only way out is by feel and through perfect familiarity with the compartment being explored. Once the light coming through the entrance hatch disappears, panic can come quickly for the untrained or inexperienced diver. Its not unusual to be completely in the dark and become entangled in debris hanging from the ceiling or protruding from the bottom. Unless a diver feels comfortable removing his equipment inside and in the dark to untangle himself from an obstruction, it is best to stay out.

The pressure hull has a length of about 160 feet and is divided above the metal flooring into six areas. They are: the forward torpedo room and crews' quarters (BUGRAUM), the wardroom and officers' quarters (OFFIZIERRAUM), the control room (ZENTRALE), the senior rates' quarters (UNTEROFFIZIERRAUM) and galley, the diesel engine room (DIESELMOTORENRAUM), and the electric motor room (E-MASCHINEN-RAUM). A seventh area, the conning tower (TURM), is located above the control room and is surrounded by its own pressure hull.

The space below the flooring is almost as large as that above it and holds the forward trim tank, torpedo compensating tanks, reserve torpedo storage space, forward and aft battery rooms, S-Gerat (sound detection equipment) compartment, magazine, fuel oil tanks, main diving tank, fresh and dirty water tanks, and aft trim tank.

Forward Torpedo Room

The forward torpedo room and crew's quarters have a length of 36 feet, are eight feet wide, and ceiling height of eight feet. It can be accessed by the forward torpedo-loading hatch. This hatch is 26 inches in diameter and offset from the deck at a 45-degree angle. It is located at the aft-end of this room and about 15 feet forward of the deck gun. The two support bars that were bolted just inside the hatch have been removed, allowing easy access to this compartment.

Until the summer of 2002, most of the forward torpedo room was filled with sand. Access to the lockers, bunks, and torpedo tubes was completely blocked by a mound of sediment that reached to within three feet of the ceiling. Only the end of the single torpedo rail could be seen about five feet inside the hatch and hanging from the ceiling.

Using an airlift dredge, most of the material in this compartment was removed over a period of several months. Along with the sediment, many artifacts were uncovered revealing much of what was stored in this room when U-85 went down. Sea boots, rain-gear, Drager lungs, goggles, life vests, and the debris from 12 bunks and three wooden tables were found in the sediment pile. The remains of 36 lockers that held the enlisted men's personal belongings still lined the walls on both sides. On the metal floor, dishes, cups, silverware and personal effects were haphazardly scattered about.

When our team reached the forward torpedo tubes in the fall of 2002, the white doors with their

identification tags still in place were seen for the first time since the sub sank in 1942. Removal of the last wall of sediment and debris was particularly exciting as the doors came into view in near-zero visibility conditions. The depth of the floor here is 105 feet.

The outboard end of the forward torpedo room is almost filled by the four 21-inch torpedo tubes. These tubes are 23 feet long and project 13 feet inside the pressure hull. There is a small walk space between the tubes that extends all the way to the forward end of the compartment. This space is still covered with sand. Three of the four tube doors are closed, but the bottom door on the port side is missing. The remains of a G7e electric torpedo protrude from this tube about four feet into the room. Why the door is gone and the torpedo is sticking out of the tube is a mystery. Numbers on the doors indicate that the top tube on the starboard side is number one, the top tube on the port side is number two, the missing door number four, and the lower starboard tube number three. The missing door may be buried in the sand below the tube.

The single rail used to load the torpedoes is still suspended from the ceiling on the port side. It makes a good guide in and out of the room when visibility is low or nonexistent. Gauges, wheels, and piping above the tubes are still in place.

During excavation of the forward torpedo room, the airlift dredge pipe had to be pulled through the forward torpedo hatch and anchored in place. This effectively blocked entrance or exit from this hatch. The pipe at times was over 80 feet long from nozzle end to discharge end. Entrance into the torpedo room by a diver had to be made via the forward battery hatch, some 20 feet away. All dives were made solo as only one person could work the dredge efficiently.

A diver's thoughts for this excursion had to be 100% focused on the job. There was no room for fear, panic or mistakes here.

One of the more recent dives made by this author into the forward torpedo room is described below.

"Entering the battery hatch, I turn on my headlight and make my way through the officers compartment to the doorway separating this area from the forward torpedo room, moving slowly and trying not to stir the sediment below me. Slipping through this narrow door, I turn right and look up to see the white 6-inch dredge pipe sticking through the forward torpedo hatch and positioned above me. The bottom here is 110 feet. Following the pipe forward, I reach the on-off lever, turn on the air, and begin work. Visibility, already close to zero, now deteriorates rapidly. My headlight illuminates enough of the pipe to see several feet into the darkness. Sand, wood, and clam shells move from the mound of sediment into the pipe. The possibility of the six-foot high mound collapsing and covering me is always on my mind. An extremely large conger eel that lives between the torpedo tubes comes out to see the action. Swimming through the light and within inches of my face-mask, the eel is content to disappear into the darkness. The suction created by the airlift is powerful enough to pull anything that comes in it's path inside the six-inch pipe, including my hand and arm. Holding the pipe with one hand, I stick my arm through the wall of muck ahead of me. I know that the number one torpedo tube can be no more than several feet away. The black cloud of sediment blocks out all light from my headlamp. My hand hits a hard object. I feel the handle on the torpedo tube door. Gripping it, I realize that this is the first time anyone has done this since that night in April of 1942 when the U-85 went down. Sliding my hand across the door, I can feel the identification tags still in place. Working with a small pocketknife, I am able to remove all but one of the tags. One corner of the large tag in the middle of the door doesn't want to let go. Checking my computer and realizing that my time is up, I leave it for the next diver.

Twenty-five minutes have passed and it's time to start the return trip. Looking back toward the torpedo hatch, the room is in total darkness. Sediment disturbed by the dredge has filled the room with tiny particles of silt. I close my eyes for a second and then open them, only to still see light from my headlamp reflecting back at me through the dense cloud of muck. The only way out is to follow the pipe to the torpedo hatch about 20 feet away. Once here, a right turn brings me back to the doorway leading into the officers quarters. Carefully and slowly moving through this door, I see sunlight shining through the battery hatch about 15 feet away. Moving up toward the opening, a large conger eel that lives in a pipe just inches below the hatch sticks his head out to give me one last scare. Pulling myself through the hatch, I check my equipment and gauges before swimming to the descent line attached to the conning tower 20 feet away.

It's early October and the water temperature is in the mid 70s. Thousands of fish, large and small swim rapidly around me and close to the hull of U-85. The warm water has attracted 15 or 20 extremely large barracuda to the wreck. The smaller fish are corralled near the bottom as the cuda patrol 60 feet above near the surface. I'll have to swim through the large cuda to reach the boat.

My first stop on the way up is the junction of the hang line and the descent line at about 30 feet. Several cuda wait motionless just above me. We make eye contact and then I move on. Being the last diver, I disconnect the hang line's large shiny clip from the descent line. As the hang line falls free and I ascend toward the next stop, one of the large barracuda, at least a six-footer, rushes forward and attacks the shiny clip, pulling it through the water several feet. Only three feet away, I'm startled but continue my ascent, reaching the 15 foot stop where I do a 20 minute hang before climbing into the boat."

On very rare occasions, barracuda like sharks and other marine animals, behave in unpredictable ways. John Finelli, an experienced diver and frequent visitor to the U-85 experienced such an unnerving incident involving a barracuda here in the summer of 2001.

As usual, we were diving alone and working the dredge in the sound room. The water was clear and warm and a large group of barracuda moved over the wreck just above the decking. Finelli reached the submarine near the conning tower and moved toward the battery hatch where he would make his entry and take his turn with the dredge. Looking toward the stern, he noticed seven or eight large barracuda about 30 feet from his location. One of the fish seemed to be agitated and moved erratically in an almost vertical position. Finelli watched the fish cautiously but still didn't anticipate what was about to happen. Suddenly, the barracuda charged Finelli, covering the 25 or 30 feet in a flash. John instinctively lifted his tool bag in front of his face, just an instant before the fish slammed into it. Startled, Finelli watched as the cuda returned to the group, still twitching and acting very agitated.

This was enough for John, who returned to the descent line and headed for the surface. Unknown to him, it wasn't over yet. Reaching the 20-foot hang line below the boat, Finelli relaxed and peered down into the blue water. Suddenly, the barracuda rocketed straight up from the depths, passing several feet beneath John and then plunging back down

and out of sight. Not waiting to see what would happen next, Finelli swam to the ladder and crawled onto the boat's swim platform. No more sub diving for John that day.

Fully loaded, ten torpedoes, four of which are still in the tubes, almost completely filled the forward torpedo room. Four torpedoes are still stored under the deck plates but the two that were suspended from the ceiling are gone. They were loaded into the forward tubes replacing those fired April 10th, 1942 at the *Christine Knudson*. Torpedoes had to be maneuvered into the submarine through the forward torpedo hatch, and were moved about in the compartment using a hoist, which ran on the rail along the roof. Five men working together loaded the torpedoes into the tubes.

Most of the crew lived and slept in the forward torpedo room although there were only 12 bunks. Twenty-seven crewmen of all duties shared some or most of their daily routines in the forward compartment.

Wardroom And Officers' Quarters

The next area, the wardroom and officers' quarters, is about 24 feet long and is accessible via the forward battery hatch. This hatch cover was removed several years ago, opening the area to dredging and exploration. The space is separated from the forward torpedo room by a thin metal bulkhead and a rectangular hatchway. The compartment at one time included: a head and washroom, chief petty officers' bunks and storage lockers, wardroom and officers' area, sound room and radio room, and the Captain's quarters. Nine men lived in this compartment.

Remnants of the head, one of two on the U-boat, are located on the port side, aft of the dividing metal bulkhead between this compartment and the forward torpedo room. It is mostly filled with sand and has given up a wooden toilet seat, valves, and several porcelain faucets. Next came four bunks, two on each side for the four chief petty officers. These bunks as well as the storage cabinets and lockers are gone. This area was airlifted many years ago and produced a variety of interesting artifacts. What's left of the food storage cabinet across from the head is still recognizable, although all items stored here have long since disappeared. Quite a bit of sand remains on the port side of this area where the mess table and two bunks were located. The remains of four lockers on the wall of the starboard side are easily recognized beside the food storage cabinet. The bottom here is 110 feet at the deepest point.

The officers' area is just aft of this space and was separated from the CPOs' by a thin wooden bulkhead and hatch. This bulkhead does not exist today. Two bunks were located on each side next to the pressure hull for the four officers as were the bunks for the CPOs. A permanent mess and worktable on the port side of the officers area allowed this space to double as the boat's wardroom. This area has also been dredged. It produced among other things, a complete set of navigational books and many personal items belonging to the officers. Nothing recognizable exists here today. It is the easiest area to explore in the sub, located just below and forward of the forward battery hatch. All of the interior walls are gone leaving one large room. On good days, it is well lighted and easy to enter and exit.

Each of the officers and CPOs had a private bunk, the ultimate status symbol on a submarine. There was no real privacy however for the chiefs and officers and, as with all accommodations other than the Captain's, there was a constant stream of men passing thru the main hallway.

On the port side and aft of the officer's area, the Captain's accommodation occupied the only really private space on the U-boat. A curtain screened off this compartment from the rest of the submarine. Neither walls nor screens define this area today. A metal post extending from ceiling to floor just aft of the battery hatch was the outside corner of the Captain's quarters. This post separates the narrow hallway from the Captain's area. A diver must pass to the left or right of this obstruction to reach the radio room or control rooms. The right passage seems to be the safest. A large water tank across from this post was the base for the Captain's bed. Today the tank is home for one of the many conger eels living within the pressure hull. Everything else that originally defined the room is gone.

The radio and sound rooms are located across from the Captains accommodation and forward of the control room. The sound room is forward and the radio room aft adjacent to the control room. Both of the narrow entrance doors are gone.

The narrow hallway between these rooms has given up many interesting artifacts over the years. The largest recovery of dishes, cups, silverware, and other crockery was discovered here just below the battery hatch and on the starboard side next to the sound room. A dredging operation in 1998 uncovered this mother lode of crockery, which netted over 50 items. Additional sand removal cleared the hallway between the control room and the officers' quarters and made exploration of these areas possible.

Another find, an unarmed G7H magnetic firing torpedo pistol still in its carrying container, was located in the hallway between the Captain's room and the radio room, during the summer of 2000. This pistol, used on twin-bladed G7e electric torpedoes was probably being readied for the nose of the spare fish in the stern torpedo room just before U-85 was sunk. The torpedo in the stern tube had just been fired at the rapidly closing *Roper*.

The pistol was first discovered sticking out of the sand with only the small propeller showing. A circular metal basket seemed to surround it. This was later found to be it's carrying container. The aggregate composition of material covering the warhead resembled cement and could not be dug into. At first it appeared that it would be impossible to pry this object loose.

Finally after many tries, an ingenious plan was devised by Roger Hunting to free the pistol. A com-a-long would be carried inside through the forward battery hatch and attached with rope to piping along the ceiling. A cable would be threaded through the container holding the pistol. This cable would then be shackled together and attached to the com-a-long. All of this had to be done in a very narrow space in the darkness.

It worked on the first try. Two divers, Roger Hunting, and myself did the job in about 30 minutes. The 40-pound object was pulled out of the cement like bottom and shoved thru the battery hatch onto the deck. It was then attached to a lift bag by Rich Hunting and sent to the surface. The whole operation took only two dives.

Another interesting area below this hallway is the U-boats magazine. This space, eight-feet long, eight-feet deep and four feet wide was located below a 19-inch by 19-inch hatch cover directly between the radio room and the Captain's room. When the cover was removed during the summer of 2001, it was discovered that the magazine was completely filled with sand. Only the top rungs of the latter leading down into the compartment were visible.

Airlifting the sand from this room took several weeks. On the ceiling of the room just starboard of the ladder, a brass cage light with glass and bulb still intact, was soon discovered. After several feet of sand were removed, lines of 88mm. shells in their storage containers filling both ends of the room came into view. Over 200 of these shells were found here. The shells in the containers are 36 inches long, leaving only two feet of clearance down the middle of the room. Above the 88.mm shells and on any open wall space, wooden storage shelves lined the compartment. Besides the 88.mm shells, other ordinance discovered included: four boxes of 20mm. rounds, six boxes of brass flares, several 9mm. drums for the MG-34 heavy machine gun, and two boxes of 9mm. rounds, packed 1500 to a box. Several boxes of tools for working on the torpedoes and deck guns were also found. A spare gun sight for the 88mm. deck gun, cleaning equipment for this gun, a torpedo firing calculator, one machine gun, and a spare barrel for the 20mm. deck cannon rounded out the items in the magazine.

Recovery of the spare barrel proved to be almost fatal for one diver. The barrel was in a capped container and attached to an inaccessible metal post inside the magazine. All attempts to remove the cylinder from the outside were fruitless. This diver, who spent the best part of a week trying to remove the container decided to try the com-a-long method used to dislodge the torpedo pistol. The com-a-long was again tied to piping on the ceiling of the pressure hull and then attached to the container holding the barrel. After several cranks on the com-a-long, the ceiling piping came crashing down on top of the diver who was momentarily trapped. Visibility went to zero as rapid silting occurred. The diver, who was one of the most experienced members of group, kept a cool head and was able to navigate under the massive piping, past the battery hatch that was now blocked, through the door into the forward torpedo room, and out the forward torpedo hatch. Several days later, the piping was secured to the ceiling by several ropes, re-opening the hallway and access to the sound and radio rooms.

To successfully work in the magazine, a diver's equipment had to be modified to include an octopus with a 15-foot hose. The diver would enter the battery hatch, remove his B. C. and tank and place it in the control room. Then, breathing from the octopus on the long hose, he would enter the magazine and work. Depths in the magazine reached more than 110 feet. Due to the sub's list, the danger of the 40-pound rounds slipping and trapping a diver inside was always a possibility. After 25 or so minutes of work, the diver would slip out through the small hatch, re-assemble his equipment, and exit the sub. These dives were also done solo as only one person could work at the time.

The radio and sound rooms were filled with sand, all the way to their ceilings before the summer of 2001. Both of these rooms are extremely small and difficult to enter. One of the main obstacles keeping divers out of the radio room was the control room door. This circular door was open and blocked the entrance into the radio room. An attempt to close the door by Roger Hunting resulted in its falling away from the control room bulkhead and almost on top of Roger. This was fair warning to the divers that structures inside U-85, although almost indestructible 60 years before could fall and trap a diver with little or no warning.

Today both of these rooms are empty of sand and reveal much of the radio and sound equipment once used to track shipping and send coded messages. On many dives, our space in the sound room had to be shared with a large conger eel that lived here. The eel would usually move out when one of

the divers peered through the small doorway. On one occasion, the eel, about seven feet long with a head at least five inches across would not leave. Picking up a short piece of wood lying in the hallway, Rich Hunting carefully encouraged the conger to leave by poking it in the face. The eel, irritated by all of this, snapped the board into and quickly exited the room.

The ships chronometer was found in this room by another team of divers. The chronometer was wedged under the remains of a wooden counter attached to the bulkhead separating the sound and radio rooms. This valuable clock was in a wooden box contained in another slightly larger box. The opening of both boxes on the surface was one of the most exciting moments I've experienced diving the U-85.

Our most important discovery in the radio room was the four rotor Enigma M2946 and a printing device-a modified typewriter-which appears to have been connected to M2946. Rich and Roger Hunting and myself accomplished this feat. A partial description of the recovery operation follows in a letter from Roger Hunting to Enigma expert David Hamer.

"We found the *enigma* on July 3, 2001. We began running an air-lift dredge operation inside the U-85 during the summer of 2000. This past summer we concentrated our efforts in the Radio Room and Sound Room. In June we spent a week emptying out the Sound Room (we did that first since it was easiest to reach). It took three divers about six days to pump out the Sound Room at 2-3 dives each per day, 30-35 minutes per dive (about 20 hours of continuous dredging). We found lots of little artifacts in the Sound Room, probably the most significant was a large brass compass, and a wooden box of phonograph records and the stack of *enigma* log sheets.

We then moved to the Radio Room, which was considerably more difficult to dredge because of it's location and the volume of debris to be removed. On the third day of dredging, we uncovered the *enigma* (M2946) lying on the floor about in the center of the room. The wooden lid was not on the box when we found it. We found the printer contraption on the same day, in about the same location. Two days later, we found the lid of the box and the wheels for what appears to be the second machine (M3131). We spent another week or so cleaning the Radio Room and found a couple of coffee cups, a Perrier water bottle, a flashlight, two ceramic insulators used on the external radio antenna and other miscellaneous junk.

Our U-boat excursion of July 3rd started like most of the others. On the way out from Thicket Lump Marina on Rog's boat *Free Flow*, the three of us reviewed our plans for the day's diving. We would work in the radio room and be on the lookout for an *enigma* machine. We knew that if this machine was still on board, it would probably be somewhere in this room. U-boat commanders had standing orders to pitch these machines overboard if capture or sinking in shallow water was imminent. This was certainly what Greger faced while being pursued by the destroyer *Roper*. We had no way of knowing whether he did this or not.

We picked up our mooring buoy about 7:30 and soon had the 150-foot air hose from the boat's compressor overboard and our descent and hang lines in place. Rog would dive first, Rich second, and me third. Roger rolled off the boat around 8:00. Using a 120 steel cylinder and a 36% nitrox mix, he planned to return in about 40 minutes. Rich gave him about three minutes to attach the air hose to the dredge pipe that was already inside the radio room, and started the compressor. When a large plume of air bubbles broke the surface several minutes later, we knew that the dredge was working properly.

After discussing our dive plans, Rich gathered his equipment and suited up. He would begin his dive about 10 minutes before Roger was due back. Doing a back roll off the transom, he disappeared below the boat about 8:30.

Alone on the boat, I moved to the bow and watched Larry Keens dive boat *Gekos*, make it's way toward another mooring over the sub. It wasn't long before I heard Roger calling for me. I could barely hear him over the roar of the air compressor. I made my way toward the stern to see what he needed. Looking over the transom and down into the water, I saw Roger holding on to the dive ladder with one hand and clinging to a wooden box with the other. He was very exhausted and barely able to keep his head up. I climbed over the stern onto the swim platform and took the box from Roger's grasp. It was the *enigma* machine we had been looking for.

Rog climbed on board, removed his dive gear, and then began telling me how he recovered this remarkable find. He had worked for 20 minutes or so, removing sediment from the radio room. After checking his computer and finding that he had only several minutes of bottom time remaining, he stuck his free hand into the mud as far as he could reach. To his amazement, he felt what he believed was the corner of a box. Dropping the dredge pipe, he used both hands to grip the box and free it from the mud. Holding the box close to his headlight, he could not identify what he had found.

Lifting the object out of the radio room, Rog tucked the box under his arm and moved through the haze toward the dim light coming through the battery hatch. Just as he passed the Captain's room, Rich came sliding through the battery hatch and faced him in the hallway. Rich, not knowing what his brother had found continued past him toward the radio room. Roger, who was now right below the battery hatch, lifted the 40-pound *enigma* up and through the opening onto the deck. Pulling himself through the hatch, he was able to see the *enigma* in the sunlight and realized what it was.

Roger decided to carry the *enigma* to the surface rather than leaving it for the next diver (me) to send up with a lift bag. Other divers were beginning to appear on the sub and the *enigma* was too valuable to leave unattended. Crawling across the deck and up on top of the conning tower, Rog fully inflated his Buoyancy Compensator. This additional 30 pounds of lift was not enough to move him and the machine from the wreck. So with great difficulty, he pulled himself up the line with one hand and held the machine, cradled under his arm, with the other. The *enigma* machine and Roger were both on the boat 10 minutes later.

At a private gathering in Hatteras on November 2nd, 2002, the M2946 four rotor *enigma* and typewriter were given to the Graveyard of the Atlantic Museum by Roger Hunting, Rich Hunting, Jim Bunch, Billy Daniels and the German Government. The machine and other artifacts from the U-85 will be restored and placed on display at the museum soon.

In a letter to each of us, Joseph K. Schwarzer, II, Executive Director and CEO of the Graveyard of the Atlantic Museum, had this to say. "On behalf of the Board of Directors and Staff of the Graveyard of the Atlantic Museum, please accept my thanks for your thoughtful and generous donation of the Naval *Enigma* Machine Type M4 Serial #2946 and the associated printer. Your vision and sense of community service in making this valuable historic artifact available to the general public, through the Graveyard of the Atlantic Museum, sets a standard for wreck divers throughout the nation. You have retrieved these artifacts from oblivion and contributed significantly to preserving the maritime history of North Carolina's Outer Banks."

Control Room

The control room, about 20 feet long and 16 feet wide with an eight-foot ceiling, occupies the center of the submarine. It is separated from the rest of the boat by a pressure bulkhead at each end. On all occasions except during an attack, the boat was controlled from this room. During an attack, the Captain controlled the U-boat from the conning tower where he would call down his instructions through a voice tube to the officers below.

Entry into the control room can be accomplished by swimming through the circular hatchway located about 15 feet aft of the forward battery hatch. As previously mentioned, the 42-inch forward circular door to the control room fell from it's hinges and is lying in the sand. Although dredging has been attempted in this compartment, it has been unsuccessful due to the cement-like mixture of clamshells and sand covering the floor.

Once through the hatchway, the first structure encountered is the sky periscope mast extending up and through the ceiling. This periscope, used mainly for navigation, could only be used from the control room and was not used during daylight-submerged attacks because the large head could be spotted easily cutting through the water. The body of the periscope and periscope well are buried under several feet of aggregate composed mostly of clamshells that fill the entire control room. The head of this periscope was removed (sawed off) by divers in the mid-seventies.

Turning to the left, the steering station on the bulkhead next to the circular hatch and the gyro compass and the two engine telegraphs that were located above it are gone. The large wheels for operating the forward diving tanks are still above the hatch. The two plainsmen's stations and hydroplane controls located along the starboard pressure hull are below the level of the sediment and not visible. The three-inch shell that exploded inside this room knocked out all of the glass gauges above this station.

A large well in the center of the room houses the attack periscope mast. This periscope has a much smaller head lens than the sky periscope and could only be used from the conning tower. Beside the well and forward of it, the cylindrical entrance to the conning tower is only several feet above the bottom, indicating the large amount of sediment in this room.

To the right of this well, the remains of the container that held the master gyrocompass is tangled in the metal debris rearranged by the explosion of *Roper's* three-inch shell. The large ballast pumps that were located near the aft control room bulkhead are not recognizable. This is as far as a diver can go. Sunlight shines through the gaping hole in the pressure hull just inside and above the aft control room doorway. Debris fills the space in front of the doorway preventing entrance into the next compartment, the petty officers' quarters.

Moving back and around the large periscope well, and looking up through the barrel like tube that extends through the ceiling of the control room and leads to the conning tower, light shines through the towers access hatch 15 feet above. It is impossible to exit from the control room through this hatch with equipment on. The access tube is too narrow to accommodate a diver with tanks. In an emergency, a diver could remove his tanks and either push them ahead or drag them behind him and leave the sub by this route.

Conning Tower

This tiny compartment about seven feet tall and attached to the pressure hull contained the equipment needed to aim the boats torpedoes. These were the compass repeater, the attack computer, and the attack periscope. Entry into the conning tower can be made through the conning tower hatch or through the control room-ceiling hatch.

About half full of sand the conning tower is very difficult to work in. All of the gauges and instruments that were attached to the walls of this compartment are either gone or buried. Entering the conning tower with dive equipment in place is risky and not very rewarding. Most everything can be seen from the outside by shinning a light through the conning tower hatch.

Senior Rates' Quarters

Behind the control room, the senior rates' quarters and galley extend the interior of the pressure hull another 22 feet. This area was also known as the *Leipzigerstrasse*, or grand central station area because it was so heavily traveled. Four bunks on each side of the passageway and two collapsible dining tables once filled this compartment. The remainder of the crew lived here, two men sharing each bunk. Two folding wooden tables were stored under the bunks and set up for dining. Lockers were located behind the bunks for personal storage. Berths, like those of the enlisted men, were shared. Their occupants however enjoyed the advantages of permanent fixtures and more headroom. Since the path through this compartment carried the most daily traffic, everyone moving from the control room to the galley, the engine room and the electric motor and aft torpedo room passed through here. The compartment is also very narrow due to the internal fuel oil bunkers on both sides.

The galley was at the aft end of the senior rates' quarters and was very small. Here, the cook or smutje prepared hot meals for 45 men with nothing more than three-or-four hot plates, a small oven, a soup kettle, and a sink. The aft head took up the port side of the galley space.

The galley hatch, located about ten feet behind the aft battery-loading hatch, is the best access point to reach these areas. The rectangular aft battery hatch is right above the senior rates' compartment but is very small and can only be used as an entry point if tanks are left outside and an umbilical hose is used for the air supply.

Dredging has been done in both the galley and senior rates' quarters. The lockers, tables, bunks, and crockery are mostly gone. The small battery hatch was removed several years ago giving access to the forward end of the senior rates' area and opened an escape route if the other hatch became blocked. The dredge pipe could be pushed through the small battery hatch and divers would enter through the galley hatch to work. Many dinner plates and coffee cups have been found below the sediment and debris here.

Before this hatch was opened, working in the galley area or senior rates' quarters required a diver to pull the dredge pipe in behind him, leaving no escape exit. One diver, working in this manner, tried to clear the pipe with his hand after it became clogged with debris. The suction pulled his hand and about half of his arm up into the pipe. He now found himself inside the galley area alone; arm stuck in the pipe, and no way out unless he could either dislodge his arm or push the pipe with his arm in it out through the galley hatch. He switched the air off at the nozzle but still could not pull his arm free. Finally, he was able to push the heavy pipe with his arm still in it, out through the hatch. The diver and

the pipe ended up on the bottom below the galley hatch in the sand. The suction inside the pipe finally decreased enough for him to free his arm and swim for the ascent line. Back on the boat he made the comment "next time you plan to do this again, let me know, so I can stay home."

Once inside the galley hatch, the remains of the oven and stove are just to port. These structures are attached to a thin bulkhead separating the galley from the engine room. The wooden partition that separated the galley from the senior rates' quarters is gone. Looking forward along the port side, a large compressed air cylinder hangs dangerously above the floor. The possibility of this bottle coming loose and rolling across the compartment floor, trapping anyone in its way, is something to consider before entering this area. Sand and sediment cover the starboard side obscuring the remnants of bunks and lockers. Everything on the port side has fallen down and litters the central hallway.

Moving forward the entire length of the compartment, the open after control room hatch is blocked on the outside by debris filling the aft end of the control room. Pipes and cables here hang loosely from the overhead. Turning around and heading back toward the galley hatch, light from the small battery hatch is a good guide, letting the diver know where he is.

Diesel Engine Room

Aft of the galley behind a metal bulkhead and open rectangular door, the diesel engine room continues another 24 feet. The diesel engine room still houses the two diesels that provided surface propulsion for the U-boat, one on each side of a narrow walkway. These engines occupy virtually the entire compartment. This room is accessible through the rectangular doorway just below the galley hatch.

The Diesel engine room has never been dredged, and sand has accumulated here almost to the ceiling.

Looking through this doorway, the tops of the two diesel engines and their overhead gauge panels can be recognized. Movement into this room is very restricted due to the extreme accumulation of sand. Penetration farther than five or six feet is very dangerous. It is impossible to turn around once in this area and backing out is necessary. Entanglement in the wires and piping hanging from the ceiling is almost certain. It's a good room to stay out of.

Electric Motor And Stern Torpedo Room

The final compartment is the electric motor and stern torpedo room. This space that extends 32 feet to the tip of the pressure hull, houses the stern torpedo tube, two electric motors, and electric controls and indicator panels that were used during submerged running. The single 23-foot tube launched it's torpedo between the two rudder blades. A torpedo from this tube was fired at the *Roper* the night of the sinking. The reserve torpedo is probably still below the deck plates. Torpedoes were loaded into this area through the stern torpedo-loading hatch. The emergency steering station is also located near the aft-end of this compartment.

Entry into this room is all but impossible. It has never been dredged or even entered by more than a few feet. Sand fills the room to within a foot of the ceiling. Two horizontal bars block the torpedo hatch from the inside. These bars are removable and strengthened the hull when the boat was submerged. Divers have penetrated this area with an umbilical hose, leaving all equipment on the outside. This is extremely dangerous and presents a serious entanglement problem. Back in the early 1980s I was on board the dive boat *Sea Fox* when a

diver tried to enter this compartment. He tried this by removing his tank, sliding between the bars, and then pulling his tank in behind him. He got in all right but got stuck on the way out. After returning to the *Sea Fox* in a panicked state, this diver, who was very experienced and had dived the U-85 many times before, recounted to the rest of us how he almost lost his life trying this foolish maneuver.

Afterword

The dives just described are synoptic of the dives made by this writer on and inside the U-85 over the past 22 years. The majority of these dives were made during June, July, August, or September. Visibility on the wreck was best during periods of light southwest winds and low swells, although optimum conditions below 60 feet are never totally predictable due to the constant movements of cold subsurface water masses probably associated with the Labrador Current. These water masses move continually over the wreck and totally determine what diving will be like from day-to-day. Perfect near-surface visibilities can change to near zero after passing through the thermocline separating the warm surface water mass and the cold murky bottom water.

To date, no diver has ever been lost on the U-85.

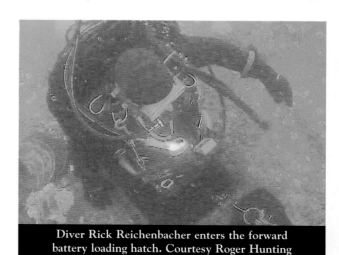
Diver Rick Reichenbacher enters the forward battery loading hatch. Courtesy Roger Hunting

Rich Hunting looks into the forward battery loading hatch. Courtesy Roger Hunting

The airlift dredge pipe extending into the magazine. Courtesy Roger Hunting

Rows of 88m. shells line the walls of the magazine. Courtesy Roger Hunting

A cage light with glass and bulb intact just below the magazine hatch. Courtesy Roger Hunting

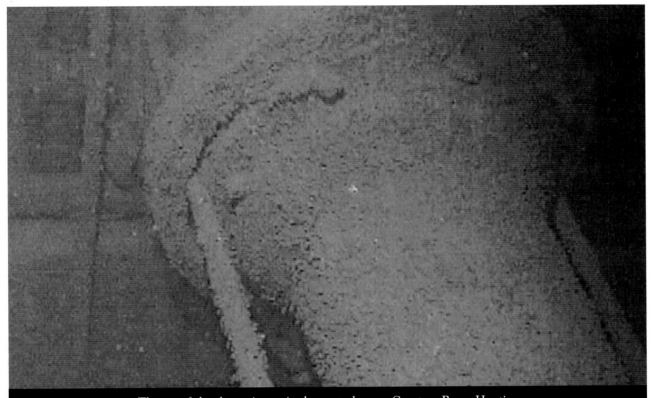

The top of the sky periscope in the control room. Courtesy Roger Hunting

A conger eel behind the sky periscope on the floor of the control room. Courtesy Roger Hunting

Recoveries

Making History Come Alive

Scuba diving provides a means for divers to enter the past, go places where few have gone, and bring back something that most likely would never have been seen again. To explore a sunken ship and recover a piece of history is an extraordinary experience that only divers know. To see pictures of and hear about the past is one thing, to touch and recover it from the bottom of the sea is another.

The U-85 shipwreck is a treasure chest of history. Much of her past is still held inside her steel shell. Many mysteries, including exactly how she sank and what happened to her Captain are still there.

Unfortunately, the shell protecting these secrets is dissolving in the seawater that has been U-85's home for more than 50 years. When the shell is gone, everything inside will be gone too, scattered about or buried forever beneath the ocean floor. Only the artifacts recovered by divers will remain to tell U-85's story.

The following pages are filled with pictures of recovered artifacts from the U-85. Access to most of these required entry into the submarine's pressure hull. Only through extensive training, long hours of planning, strict adherence to safety procedures and teamwork, were the divers able to successfully bring these artifacts to the surface. The smiles on their faces reveal some of the excitement felt after returning to the surface with their piece of history.

Gekos divers display china recovered from the U-85.

A small shot glass and badge recovered by Billy Hade.

Marty Bailey with china recovered from the senior rates' quarters.

Dan Irvin with the U-boats chronometer.

Rich Hunting with a recovered MP-40 machine gun.

Roger Hunting holds a torpedo calculator recovered from the magazine.

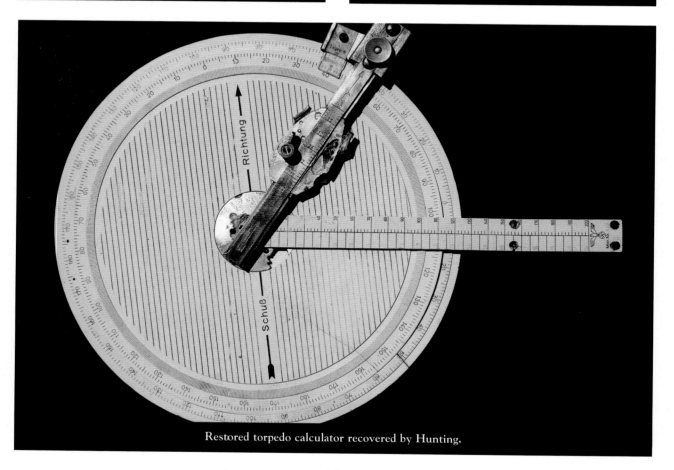

Restored torpedo calculator recovered by Hunting.

Jim Bunch holds an 88mm. round still in it's storage canister.

John A. Watkins with 88mm. round for the deck gun.

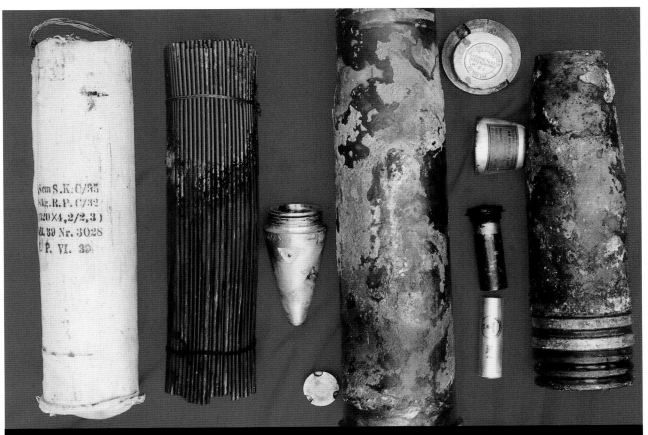

Disassembled 88mm. deck gun artillery shell.

Roger Hunting just after recovering the
four rotor marine *Enigma* machine M2946.

M3131 *Enigma* machine recovered and restored by Roger Hunting.

Hunting recovered the Naval Enigma Machine Type M4, serial number 2946 and associated printer on July 3, 2001.

Gun sight for the 88mm. deck gun recovered from U-85's magazine and restored by Roger Hunting.

Ornate tool box with tools for working on the 88mm. deck gun recovered and restored by Roger Hunting .

Selected Bibliography

Books

Bagnasco, Erminio. Submarines of World War Two. Naval Institute Press, 1977.
Beaver, Paul. U-boats in the Atlantic. Cambridge, 1979.
Breyer, Siegfried, and Koop, Gerhard. The U-boat. Schiffer Publishing, 1987.
Buchheim, Gunther. U-boat War. Bonanza Books, 1986.
Blair, Clay, Jr. Hitlers U-boat War. Vols. 1 & 2, Random House, 1997.
Bottling, Douglas. The U-boats. Time-Life Books, 1979.
Bunch, Jim. Diving the U-85. Deep Sea Press 1986.
Busch, Rainer, and Roll, Hans-Joachim. German U-boat Commanders of World War II. Greenhill Books, 1999.
Caram, Ed. U-352: The Sunken German U-bcat in the Graveyard of the Atlantic. 1987.
Cheatham, James T. The Atlantic Turkey Shoot: U-boats off the Outer Banks in World War Two. Williams and Simpson. 1990.
Chewning, Alpheus J. The Approaching Storm: U-boats off the Virginia Coast During World War II. Brandylane Publishers, 1994.
Cremer, Peter. U-boat Commander. Naval Institute Press, 1984.
Donitz, Admiral Karl. Memoirs: Ten Years and Twenty Days. Leisure Books, 1959.
Edwards, Beernard. Donitz and the Wolf Packs. Brockhampton Press, 1999.
Farb, Roderick. Shipwrecks: Diving the Graveyard of the Atlantic. Menaska Ridge Press, 1985.
Fargo, Ladislas. The Tenth Fleet. Sarah Jennings, 1962.
Gannon, Michael. Black May. Dell Publishing, 1998.
Gannon, Michael. Operation Drumbeat. Harper and Row, 1990.
Gasaway, E. B. Grey Wolf, Grey Sea. Ballantine Books, 1970.
Gentile, Gary. Track of the Grey Wolf. Avon Books, 1989.S
Gentile, Gary. Shipwrecks of North Carolina (North). Gary Gentile Productions, 1993.
Giese, Otto, and Wise, James. Shooting the War. Naval Institute Press, 1944.
Heinz, Karl, and Schmeelke, Michael. German U-boat Bunkers: Yesterday and Today. Schiffer. 1999.
Hickam, Homer H. Torpedo Junction. Naval Institute Press, 1989.
Hoyt, Edwin P. U-boats Offshore. Stein and Day, 1978.
Hoyt, Edwin P. U-boats: A Pictorial History. McGraw-Hill, 1987.
Hogel, Georg, U-boat Emblems of World War II 1939-1945. Schiffer, 1999.
Hughes, Terry, and Costello, John. The Battle of the Atlantic. Dial Press, 1977.
Irving, David. The Destruction of Convoy PQ17. Simon and Schuster, 1968.
Jones, Geoffrey. Defeat of the Wolfpacks. William Kimber & Company, 1986.
Kahn, David. Seizing the Enigma. Houghton Mifflin Company, 1991.
Kaplan, Philip, and Currie, Jack. Wolfpack: U-boats at War 1939-1945. Naval Institute Press, 1997.
Keatts, Henry, and Farr, George. Dive Into History: U-boats. Pices Books, 1994.
Kutta, Timothy. U-Boat War. Squadron/Signal Publications. 1998.
Macintyre, Donald. The Naval War Against Hitler. Scribner's Sons, 1971.
Mason, David. U-boat, the Secret Menace. Ballantine Books, 1969.
Miller, David. U-boats: The Illustrated History of the Raiders of the Deep. Pegasus Publishers, Ltd., 2000.
Mulligan, Timothy P. Lone Wolf: The Life and Death of U-boat Ace Werner Henke. Prager, 1993.
Mulligan, Timothy P. Neither Sharks Nor Wolves. Naval Institute Press, 1999.
Naiswald, L. VanLoan. In Some Foreign Field. John F. Blair, 1972.
Nowarra, Heinz. The German U-boat Type VII. Schiffer Publishing Ltd., 1992.
Niestle, Axel. German U-boat Losses During World War II. Naval Institute Press,1992.
Ott, Wolfgang. Sharks and Little Fishes. Ballantine Books, 1970.
Porten, Edward. The German Navy in World War II. Thomas Crowell, 1969.
Pitt, Barrie. The Battle of the Atlantic World War II. Time-Life, 1977.
Preston, Anthony. U-boats. Bison Books, 1978.
Robertson, Terrence. The Golden Horseshoe. Evans Brothers Ltd., 1955.
Roessler, Eberhard. The U-boat. Naval Institute Press, 1984.
Rohwer, Jurgen. Axis Submarine Successes, 1939-1945. Naval Institute Press, 1984.
Roscoe, Theodore. United States Destroyer Operations in World War II. Naval Institute Press, 1953.

Showell, J. P. Mallmann. U-boats Under the Swastika. Arko, 1974.

Showell, J. P. Mallmann. The German Navy in World War Two. Naval Institute Press, 1979.

Showell, J. P. Mallmann. U-boat Commanders and Crews 1935-1945. Crowood Press, 1998.

Showell, J. P. Mallmann. U-boats in Camera. Sutton Publishing, 1999.

Stern, Robert C. U-boats in Action. Squadron/Signal Publications, 1977.

Stern, Robert C. Type VII U-boats. Brockhampton Press, 1991.

Stick, David. Graveyard of the Atlantic. University of North Carolina Press, 1952.

Stick, David. The Outer Banks of North Carolina. University of North Carolina Press, 1958.

Savas, Theodore P. Silent Hunters: German U-boat Commanders of World War II. Savas Publishing Company, 1977.

Tarrant, V. E. The U-boat Offensive 1914-1945. Naval Institute Press, 1989.

Terraine, John. The U-boat Wars 1916-1945. Henry Holland Company, 1989.

Topp, Eric. The Odyssey of a U-boat Commander: Recollections of Eric Topp. Prager 1992.

U-boat Commanders Handbook. Thomas Publications, 1989.

Vause, Jordan. U-boat Ace: The Story of Wolfgang Luth. Naval Institute Press, 1990.

Vause, Jordan. Wolf: U-boat Commanders in World War II. Naval Institute Press, 1997

Waters, Captain John M. USCG Retired. Bloody Winter. Naval Institute Press, 1984.

Werner, Herbert A. Iron Coffins. Holt, Rinehart, & Winston, 1969.

Westwood, David. The Type VII U-boat. Naval Institute Press, 1984.

Wiggins, Melanie. U-boat Adventures. Naval Institute Press, 1999.

Wynn, Kenneth. U-boat Operations of the Second World War Vol. I. Naval Institute Press, 1997.

Unpublished Material

National Archives II, Adelphi, Maryland

Record Group 38

The records of the Office of Naval Intelligence, located among the Records of the Chief of Naval Operations, Record Group 38, include several sources of information. The records of Office Op-Z, responsible during World War II for intelligence about German U-boat activities, includes copies of paper records and personal effects recovered from the bodies of U-85 crewmen, as well as detailed data on the identification and interment of the remains of the U-85 crew.

Records of the Tenth Fleet

Among the records of the U. S. Tenth Fleet, which coordinated antisubmarine operations during the war, there is a detailed account of U-85's sinking by the U.S.S. Roper among the ASW Assessment Incident Files (Incident No. 400), including the Roper's own after-action report of the sinking. Finally a collection of intercepts of decrypted and translated German Navy messages includes a number of messages sent or received by the U-85 in late 1941 and early 1942.

Record Group 242

Microfilm Publication T1022, Records of the German Navy, 1850-1945. U-85's Kriegstabebuch (KTB), 7-June1941 - 8 April 1942, is reproduced on microfilm publication T1002, rolls 2931-32, as record item PG 30079/1-5. The microfilm is available in the Microfilm Research Room on the fourth floor.

Record Group 80-G

Photos of the bodies recovered from the U-85 can be found in Box 64. There are about fifty different shots, both on the Roper and in the cementary.

INDEX